AIR CAMPAIGN

NEW GUINEA 1942–43

Halting the last Japanese advance

MARK STILLE & JOHN ROGERS | ILLUSTRATED BY JIM LAURIER

OSPREY PUBLISHING
Bloomsbury Publishing Plc
Kemp House, Chawley Park, Cumnor Hill, Oxford OX2 9PH, UK
Bloomsbury Publishing Ireland Limited,
29 Earlsfort Terrace, Dublin 2, D02 AY28, Ireland
1385 Broadway, 5th Floor, New York, NY 10018, USA
E-mail: info@ospreypublishing.com
www.ospreypublishing.com

OSPREY is a trademark of Osprey Publishing Ltd

First published in Great Britain in 2025

© Osprey Publishing Ltd, 2025

All rights reserved. No part of this publication may be: i) reproduced or transmitted in any form, electronic or mechanical, including photocopying, recording or by means of any information storage or retrieval system without prior permission in writing from the publishers; or ii) used or reproduced in any way for the training, development or operation of artificial intelligence (AI) technologies, including generative AI technologies. The rights holders expressly reserve this publication from the text and data mining exception as per Article 4(3) of the Digital Single Market Directive (EU) 2019/790

A catalog record for this book is available from the British Library.

ISBN: Paperback 9781472866554; ePub 9781472866547; ePDF 9781472866561; XML 9781472866578

25 26 27 28 29   10 9 8 7 6 5 4 3 2 1

Maps by www.bounford.com
Diagrams by Adam Tooby
3D BEVs by Paul Kime
Index by Fionbar Lyons
Typeset by Amnet ContentSource Private Limited
Printed by Repro India Ltd.

Title page: see caption on p. 31.

Osprey Publishing supports the Woodland Trust, the UK's leading woodland conservation charity.

To find out more about our authors and books visit www.ospreypublishing.com. Here you will find extracts, author interviews, details of forthcoming events and the option to sign up for our newsletter.

For product safety-related questions, contact productsafety@bloomsbury.com

AIR CAMPAIGN

CONTENTS

INTRODUCTION	4
CHRONOLOGY	8
ATTACKER'S CAPABILITIES	10
DEFENDER'S CAPABILITIES	17
CAMPAIGN OBJECTIVES	24
THE CAMPAIGN	28
ANALYSIS AND CONCLUSION	89
BIBLIOGRAPHY	93
INDEX	95

INTRODUCTION

In 1942 the highly experienced IJNAF looked to extend Imperial Japan's reach far into the South Pacific. Its bomber and fighter units based at Rabaul expected to annihilate weak Allied air opposition over New Guinea. Here a Tainan Air Group Zero heads for an attack on Port Moresby in mid-1942. (Author's Collection)

The Japanese and Allies fought two air campaigns over New Guinea from early 1942 until mid-1944. In the first campaign, which is the subject of this book, the Japanese were on the offensive, pressing to make further gains in the South Pacific. Gaining strength, American and Australian air forces stopped the Japanese by early 1943 and thereafter the Allies conducted their own offensive air campaign in New Guinea. By the second campaign, the Imperial Japanese Navy Air Force (IJNAF) had given way to the Imperial Japanese Army Air Force (IJAAF) as the Allies' major antagonist. In that first major clash in the Pacific War between the IJAAF and the United States Army Air Force (USAAF), the Japanese were overwhelmed and their defense of New Guinea fatally undermined – this is the subject of the next book on the New Guinea air campaigns.

In early 1942, as its campaigns in the Philippines and Dutch East Indies (DEI) successfully wound up, Japan's Imperial General Headquarters (IGHQ) turned its attention eastward. Prewar plans called for a Pacific-wide defensive perimeter stretching from the Aleutian Islands through Midway Atoll into Oceania. Japan's specific goal in the South Pacific was to connect its defensive perimeter to resist future Allied attempts to reverse Japan's conquests in the DEI and Southeast Asia. The IGHQ saw two options for future operations in the South Pacific. The first was to extend Japan's reach through the Solomons, New Caledonia, Fiji, and Samoa. If successful, this thrust would effectively seal off Australia from air and maritime support from the United States, specifically the transport of American troops and military supplies to use Australia as a base for offensive operations. The second was to seize Port Moresby, the only major settlement on Papua New Guinea, to bring Japanese air and naval forces into a better position to support the advance into the South Pacific. By February 1942, Japan had created a major regional air and naval base complex at Rabaul on New Britain, approximately 900 miles north of Australia's major northeastern air bases, to facilitate its effort.

Japan ultimately decided to undertake air and naval operations along both these axes simultaneously, though internal disagreements persisted throughout 1942 about exactly what level of effort to mount in each area. This resulted in major, though unevenly prosecuted,

The objective of both attacker and defender, Port Moresby is pictured in the latter half of 1942. This view shows the town in the foreground and ships in Fairfax Harbor beyond, as well as seaplanes moored at far right. Through April 1943, the Japanese attacked Port Moresby-area targets 106 times. (Claringbould)

military efforts in both the Solomon Islands and New Guinea. Neither of these efforts would be easy, despite the initial weakness of the Allied forces in the region.

The initial Allied reaction to Japan's occupation of the DEI and Philippines was to prepare for the defense of Australia itself. The Australian Chiefs of Staff briefed General Douglas MacArthur in March on a plan to cede much of northern and western Australia to the Japanese while defending a line running diagonally from Brisbane to Adelaide. The following month, MacArthur was appointed Supreme Commander of Allied Forces in the Southwest Pacific Area (SWPA). In his new capacity, MacArthur chose to defend Australia in New Guinea, with an eye to later pursuing an offensive strategy in the Southwest Pacific to retake the Philippines. The major problem the defenders had was the lack of forces – air, sea, and land – with which to check the Japanese advance. The incremental addition of forces, development of suitable tactics, and implementation of an effective command structure were features of the Allied defensive effort during 1942.

Both attackers and defenders were subject to the same two related complications: the distances and the environment of the battlespace. In the case of distances, there were few adequate air bases along either of Japan's axes of effort. Without aircraft carriers available to position fighter and single-engine bomber aircraft close to the land objectives in these areas, the IJNAF was handicapped by the relatively short time its fighters flying from Rabaul had for combat. Aside from the sheer size of New Guinea itself – the world's second largest island after Greenland – the large distances from Australian bases to Japanese targets on New Guinea and around Rabaul complicated Allied planning and mission execution. Even with the antagonists later building several airfields on New Guinea as the campaign progressed, physical distances hampered air options.

As for the environment, both sides were negatively affected by the weather and the dense jungle terrain. The entire region was susceptible to major fluctuations in cloud density and altitude; tropical storm fronts formed quickly, often with sustained heavy rains. Additionally,

Kavieng
New Ireland
Bismarck Sea
Rabaul
Lakunai
Vunakanau
New Britain
Gasmata
Bougainville
NEW GUINEA
Lae
Salamaua
Bulolo
Wau
Shortland Islands
SOLOMON ISLANDS
Solomon Sea
Santa Isabel
Gulf of Papua
Gona
Sananada
Buna
Kokoda
Goodenough Island
Tulagi
Port Moresby
Guadalcanal
Taupota
Milne Bay
Samarai
Coral Sea
Cooktown
Cairns
Mareeba
Townsville
Antil Plains
Woodstock
Reid River
Bowen
Charters Towers
AUSTRALIA
Longreach
N
0
200 miles
0
200km

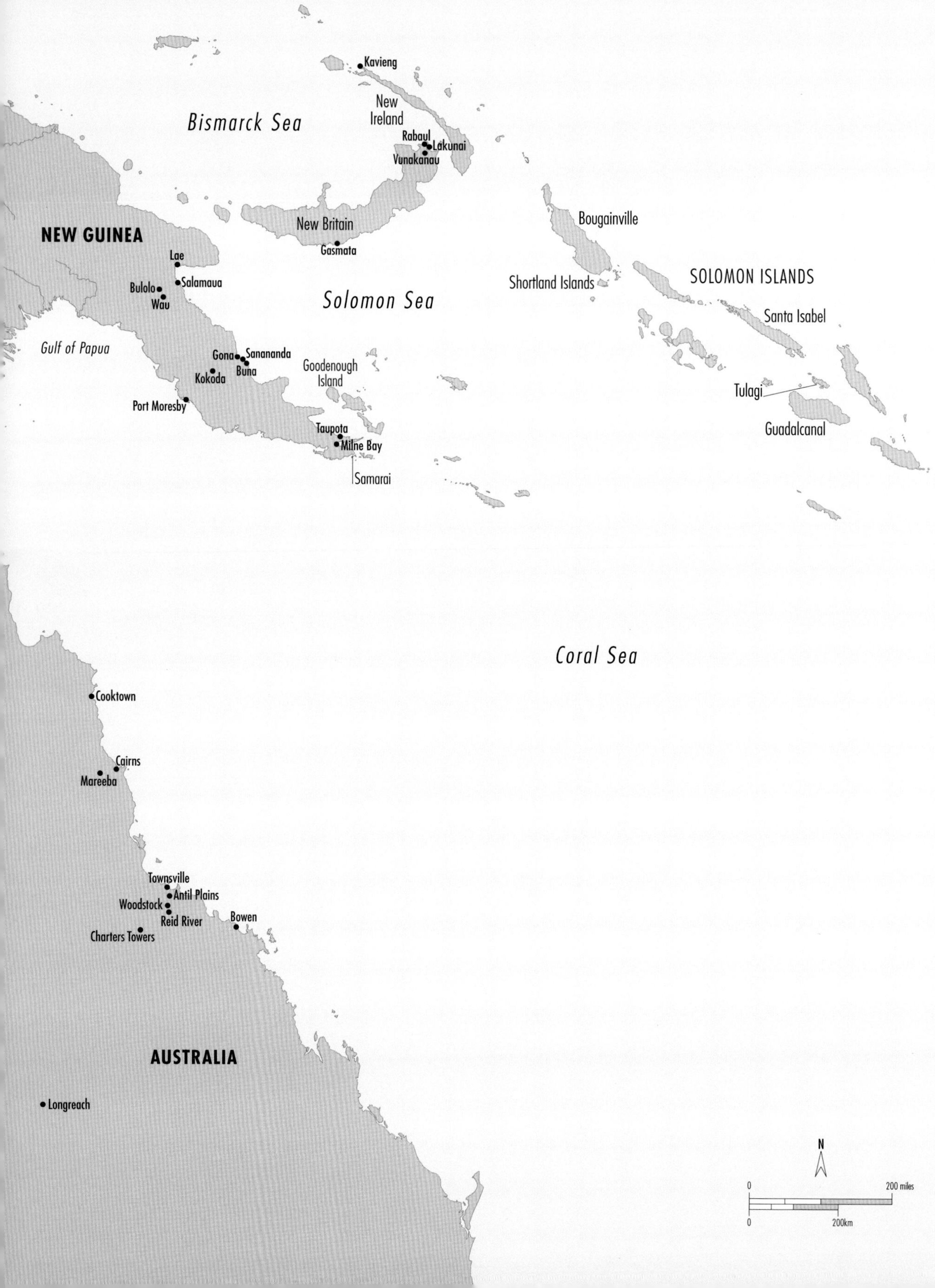

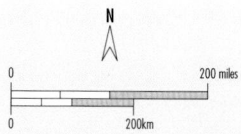

OPPOSITE MAP OF THE NEW GUINEA THEATER

accurate weather forecasting was almost impossible. All of this often made navigating long distances to targets extremely difficult, meaning targets were often obscured when they were reached. On the ground, the weather made maintenance and movement of aircraft very difficult at airfields with poor drainage and few or no permanent shelters. The jungle surrounding the bases created breeding grounds for insects carrying debilitating diseases such as malaria and dengue fever that severely afflicted personnel.

The terrain on New Guinea also presented a major obstacle. The Owen Stanley Mountains run down the middle of Papua, where the campaign was fought during 1942 and into early 1943. The 9,000–13,000ft-high range often forced aircraft crossing the mountains to follow certain routes through lower-altitude gaps in the range or climb over the range and to use more fuel, often at the expense of smaller bomb and cargo loads. The jungle covering New Guinea was in most areas virtually impenetrable and, along with shark-infested waters surrounding the island, limited the chances of survival of downed pilots, as well as the practical locations for creating new airfields.

CHRONOLOGY

1942

January 23–29 Japanese invade New Britain and quickly prepare airfields near Rabaul to receive IJNAF aircraft

February 3 First Japanese air raid on Port Moresby from Rabaul

February 23 First USAAF/RAAF (Royal Australian Air Force) combined raid on Rabaul-area targets

February 24 First combined raid by 24th Air Flotilla bombers and fighters on Port Moresby airfields

March 8 IJA South Seas Force and IJN Special Naval Landing Force troops land in northeastern New Guinea at Salamaua and Lae

March 10 Aircraft from carriers *Lexington* and *Yorktown* and USAAF and RAAF bombers attack Japanese landing force at Lae and Salamaua

March 14 First IJNAF bombing raid on northeast Australia against Horn Island airfield

March 21 RAAF No 75 Squadron Kittyhawks deploy to Port Moresby to contest Japanese air raids

April 1 25th Air Flotilla activated at Rabaul, relieving 24th Air Flotilla

April 5 First USAAF fighters based on New Guinea

April 17 First 25th Air Flotilla raid on Port Moresby

April 20 Allied Air Forces Headquarters established in Melbourne

May 7–8 Battle of the Coral Sea turns back Japanese invasion force headed for Port Moresby

June 4 Japanese suffer major defeat at the battle of Midway

June 25 Allies land garrison at Milne Bay in eastern New Guinea

July 21 Japanese 17th Army lands at Buna and begins overland push toward Port Moresby

July 22 Allies begin air attacks against Japanese ground forces and their land and maritime lines of communication in eastern New Guinea and along the Kokoda Trail; these attacks continue throughout 1942

July 29 Japanese troops advancing toward New Guinea seize Kokoda

July 30 RAAF Nos 75 and 76 Squadrons established at Milne Bay

August 3 Japanese reconnaissance flight detects Allied activity at Milne Bay

August 4 Major General George Kenney takes command of Allied Air Forces

August 7 US Marines land on Guadalcanal in the southern Solomons, forcing the Japanese to divert their main effort of air operations away from New Guinea

August 25 Battle of Milne Bay begins

September 3 USAAF 5th Air Force activated, with Kenney in command; both it and the RAAF Command fall under Kenney as commander of Allied Air Forces

September 5 Milne Bay battle ceases with evacuation of last Japanese troops

The 49th Fighter Group's 9th Fighter Squadron transitioned from P-40s to P-38s by February 1943. This development added momentum to the qualitative improvement of the 5th Air Force during the latter part of the campaign. Here a 9th Squadron P-38H gets fueled at Dobodura in April 1943, around the time of the *I-Go* attacks. (NARA)

September 15–24 5th Air Force conducts first air transport of US Army forces from Australia to Port Moresby

September 29 Australian troops go on the offensive along the Kokoda Trail

October 5 – November 2 Australian and US troops transported by air in preparation for assault on Buna from the east

November IJNAF undergoes reorganization and adds several units at Rabaul to combat Allied push to seize Buna

November 19 Allied troops attack 17th Army positions at Gona–Sanananda–Buna

November USAAF B-24Ds and P-38Fs begin operations

December 13 IJAAF fighters arrive at Rabaul

1943

January 8 Japanese resupply convoy reaches Lae, despite significant Allied air attacks

January 22 Japanese resistance at Buna ceases

January 27–30 IJA offensive stopped at Wau

March 1–4 Battle of the Bismarck Sea results in the destruction of a major Japanese Lae resupply convoy

April 7–16 Operation *I-Go* mounted against Allied New Guinea targets fails, with major Japanese losses

A 4th Air Group Betty en route to bomb Port Moresby in the first half of 1942. The Betty had decent range and carried a respectable bomb load, but was deficient in defensive armament and armor protection, suffering very high losses in the New Guinea and Solomons campaigns. (Claringbould)

ATTACKER'S CAPABILITIES
Consolidating the base

Commanders

Admiral Yamamoto Isoroku had been in command of the Imperial Japanese Navy's (IJN) Combined Fleet since before the start of the war. The Combined Fleet controlled all of the IJN's major air and naval units. As the struggle for New Guinea unfolded, Yamamoto was in the process of mismanaging the Guadalcanal campaign. His most vexing problem was trying to suppress the American airbase on Guadalcanal, failure to do so ultimately leading to Japanese defeat. Understandably, the Solomons were the focus of IJN operations, with New Guinea being a sideshow.

The 11th Air Fleet, headquartered at Rabaul, was responsible for overseeing air operations in the South Pacific. Vice-Admiral Tsukahara Nishizo assumed command of this formation in October 1941, but in August the following year he fell ill with malaria and then dengue fever. Vice-Admiral Kusaka Jinichi took over on October 8, 1942. Kusaka was not a naval aviator and had little background in aviation, but it was not unusual in the IJN for non-aviators to command aviation formations. However, he was considered an aggressive commander. On December 24, 1942, all Imperial Navy forces in the New Guinea and Solomon Islands area were combined into the newly designated Southeast Area Fleet, with Kusaka in charge. He retained this command until the end of the war.

One of the Imperial Navy's commanders associated with the New Guinea campaign was Rear Admiral Kimura Masatomi. Kimura gained flag rank in November 1942 and assumed command of Destroyer Squadron 3 at Rabaul. He commanded the Japanese convoy at the battle of the Bismarck Sea, during which his flagship sunk and he was wounded.

The Imperial Japanese Army (IJA) commander responsible for overseeing operations in New Guinea during this period was Lieutenant General Imamura Hitoshi. He assumed command of the new Eighth Area Army, with its two subordinate armies. Originally, the 17th Army was responsible for operations on New Guinea and then in the Solomon Islands when the Americans invaded there in August 1942. This was too much for a single commander, so the 18th Army was established to oversee operations on New Guinea. Imamura was promoted to general in 1943. Following the war, he was tried and convicted of war crimes.

The Imperial Japanese Navy Air Force

Beginning in August 1942 and into early 1943, the focus of IJNAF operations in the South Pacific was Guadalcanal. After that, it shifted to the central Solomons. Throughout this period, it also had to contend with persistent Allied attacks on its airfields around Rabaul. Thus, other priorities prevented the IJNAF from focusing its efforts on New Guinea, with the exception of the period from April–August 1942 and during Yamamoto's brief air offensive in April 1943. Even as the Guadalcanal campaign was winding down, the IJNAF was only capable of mounting sporadic attacks on New Guinea targets; for example, a single daylight raid on New Guinea was recorded during January 1943.

Air operations in the South Pacific were under the command of the 11th Air Fleet. The 25th Air Flotilla, established in April, assumed responsibility from the 24th Air Flotilla for operations in the Bismarck Archipelago and eastern New Guinea. It was comprised of several air groups. The 4th Air Group was composed of fighters and long-range bombers, and was quickly reinforced by bombers from the Misawa Air Group at the start of the Guadalcanal campaign. The 25th Air Flotilla's Tainan Air Group absorbed the Zeros of the original 4th Air Group. Containing several aces, it was considered the IJNAF's premier land-based fighter unit and had extensive combat experience. The 2nd Air Group was a mixed unit of short-ranged fighters and dive-bombers.

Vice-Admiral Kusaka Jinichi took over the 11th Air Fleet in October 1942 and later was given command of all Japanese forces in the South Pacific. In this role he oversaw naval operations in both the Solomons and New Guinea, but he lacked the capability to stop Allied advances in either area. (NHHC)

As the campaign for New Guinea developed into a prolonged battle of attrition, and losses mounted in the Solomons after August 7, the Japanese were forced to send more air units into the region. During a lull in September, the Japanese reorganized the air units based at Rabaul. The 25th Air Flotilla was augmented by the 26th, and all fighter, dive-bomber, and patrol aircraft were placed under the 25th; the new 26th Air Flotilla took control of all the long-range bombers. On November 10, the 25th Air Flotilla was relieved by the 21st Air Flotilla. As operations ramped up to neutralize Henderson Field on Guadalcanal, more bombers were deployed to Rabaul. Between September 16 and 23, the Kanoya and Takao Air Groups arrived at Rabaul, each with 23 long-range bombers. On September 27, the 6th Air Group, equipped with fighters, augmented the Tinian Air Group.

In October and November 1942, the IJNAF underwent a large-scale reorganization. Previously, some air groups operated multiple types of aircraft. Under the reorganization, air groups operated a single type of aircraft, and all were renumbered. The new system was orderly, but complex, so will only be outlined below:

Old designation	New designation
Fighter unit of the 2nd Air Group	582 Air Group
6th Air Group	204 Air Group
Fighter unit of the Genzan Air Group	252 Air Group
Fighter unit of the Kanoya Air Group	253 Air Group
Bomber unit of the Kanoya Air Group	751 Air Group
Misawa Air Group	705 Air Group
Tainan Air Group	251 Air Group

Rear Admiral Kimura Masatomi was charged with running the March 1943 convoy to Lae. He relied on a plan based on prior operations that were mostly successful. Kimura was unaware that the Allies had developed new tactics to make land-based airpower more deadly to ships, demonstrated in the Bismarck Sea action. (NHHC)

Shortly after this reorganization, the exhausted 251 Air Group left the South Pacific to be rebuilt. By November 1942, Zeros from the 204, 252, 253, and 582 Air Groups were available. On November 17, the 252 and 582 Air Groups moved to Lae. Two air groups with long-range bombers were also to hand. Despite the large numbers of air groups operating in the region, the 11th Air Fleet struggled to keep large numbers of aircraft operational. Typically, only some 30–40 bombers and 50–60 fighters were ready for use.

To augment their land-based air strength, the Japanese often deployed the air groups from the carriers based at Truk Atoll. It was easy to transfer carrier aircraft by air across the 820 miles from Truk to Rabaul, but Yamamoto was reluctant to do this because the carriers were a strategic asset that had to be kept ready to respond to an American advance throughout the Pacific. Exposing their air groups to attrition was something done only if the situation was critical or an important operation was being planned. When the carrier air groups were committed, success was expected since they were considered to be elite units. Examples of carrier air groups being deployed to operate from land bases in the front lines include sending most of *Hiyo*'s air group to Lae in November and using *Zuiho*'s fighter unit to cover the March convoy to Lae. In April 1943, the bulk of all four air groups of the carriers based at Truk were deployed to Rabaul for a series of massive air raids. These deployments underlined the growing weakness of the 11th Air Fleet's air units.

IJNAF aircraft

IJNAF operations over New Guinea relied almost exclusively on two types of aircraft. The first of these was the IJNAF's principal land-based medium bomber, the Mitsubishi G4M1 Navy Type 1 Attack Bomber Model 11, which later in the war received the Allied reporting name of "Betty." This book will refer to this and all other Japanese aircraft by their reporting names assigned by the Technical Air Intelligence Unit of the Far East Air Forces.

Against weak Allied opposition, the mainstay Betty enjoyed success early in the war, but when it was used to attack the well-defended American airbase at Guadalcanal and ships in the waters offshore, it suffered heavy losses. Its principal strength was an impressive range of 1,540 miles, making it capable of striking targets on New Guinea flying from Rabaul. However, this long range was gained at the expense of armor protection and self-sealing fuel tanks. On board the Betty were 1,294 gallons of fuel in wing tanks; when hit, they tended to burst into flames. Though able to carry ordnance to strike both naval and air targets, its total payload was a modest 1,760lb. Taking on an area target like an airfield, this payload proved to be inadequate. For self-protection, the Betty carried four machine guns and a tail-mounted 20mm cannon. Combined with a mediocre top speed of 231 knots at 13,800ft, the Betty was vulnerable to fighter interception.

The other principal Japanese naval aircraft active during the campaign was the IJNAF's mainstay fighter, the Mitsubishi A6M2 Model 21 Type 0 Carrier Fighter "Zeke." This and the other models of this Mitsubishi fighter will be referred to throughout this study as the "Zero." The IJNAF also operated later versions of the Zero – including the Model 22 and 32 – and did so in the same unit.

Against inferior Allied aircraft early in the war, the Zero gained a fearsome reputation. It was a truly inspired design with great range, fairly high speed, and supreme maneuverability. With a drop tank, it possessed a range of 1,200 miles, bringing all targets on New Guinea within range and giving it the ability to loiter over friendly convoys for extended periods. As well as its legendary maneuverability, the Zero possessed superior climbing capabilities and

Two Zeros sit at Lakunai airfield. Several IJNAF Zero units served during the campaign and played a major role in the 11th Air Fleet's assault on Allied airpower, escorting bombers and strafing airfields. They also flew defensive patrols over Rabaul and Lae that limited their availability for offensive tasks. (Claringbould)

good acceleration – much better than Allied fighters at the time. Its top speed of 288 knots at 14,764ft was respectable, but was inferior to some Allied counterparts. It also carried a fairly heavy armament for the period of two 20mm wing cannons and two 7.7mm machine guns mounted in the cowling. However, as was the case for the Betty, the Zero had a serious weakness: it carried almost no protective armor and no self-sealing fuel tanks, making it highly susceptible to battle damage. Another limitation of the Zero was the lack of a reliable radio that precluded nonvisual air-to-air communication and air-to-ground communication, which could have proved tactically useful.

The Mitsubishi A6M3 Navy Type 0 Carrier Model 32 "Hamp" (referred to here as the "Zero" or "A6M3") variant saw action during the New Guinea campaign. It was fitted with a more powerful engine but had a reduced fuel capacity. Accordingly, it was deployed to Lae and Buna or used in defense of Rabaul.

Of lesser importance was the IJNAF's standard dive-bomber, the Aichi D3A1 Navy Type 99 Carrier Bomber Model 11 "Val." Both carrier- and land-based units operated this aircraft. Though a stable and accurate dive-bomber, it was hampered by its small payload and vulnerability to interception. By the fall of 1942, the D3A2 variant began to reach the South Pacific. Fitted with a more powerful engine, it possessed a slightly higher maximum speed, 232 knots. However, both variants needed drop tanks to strike targets on New Guinea flying from Rabaul. Also participating periodically in the campaign was the Mitsubishi G3M Navy Type 96 Model 21 "Nell" Attack Bomber. It was an older design that was obsolescent by 1942, but was still effective against limited Allied opposition. It carried 1,764lb of bombs, mounted externally along the belly, and had a range of 3,871 miles.

The Imperial Japanese Army Air Force

During the period covered in this book, the IJNAF carried almost the entire burden of air operations in the South Pacific. Having to support operations in the Solomons and New Guinea concurrently was unsustainable, so the IJN requested help from the IJA. The first request came in late August 1942, but was rebuffed by the IJAAF. There was good reason for this refusal. Simply put, the IJAAF was not trained for, nor did it plan to conduct,

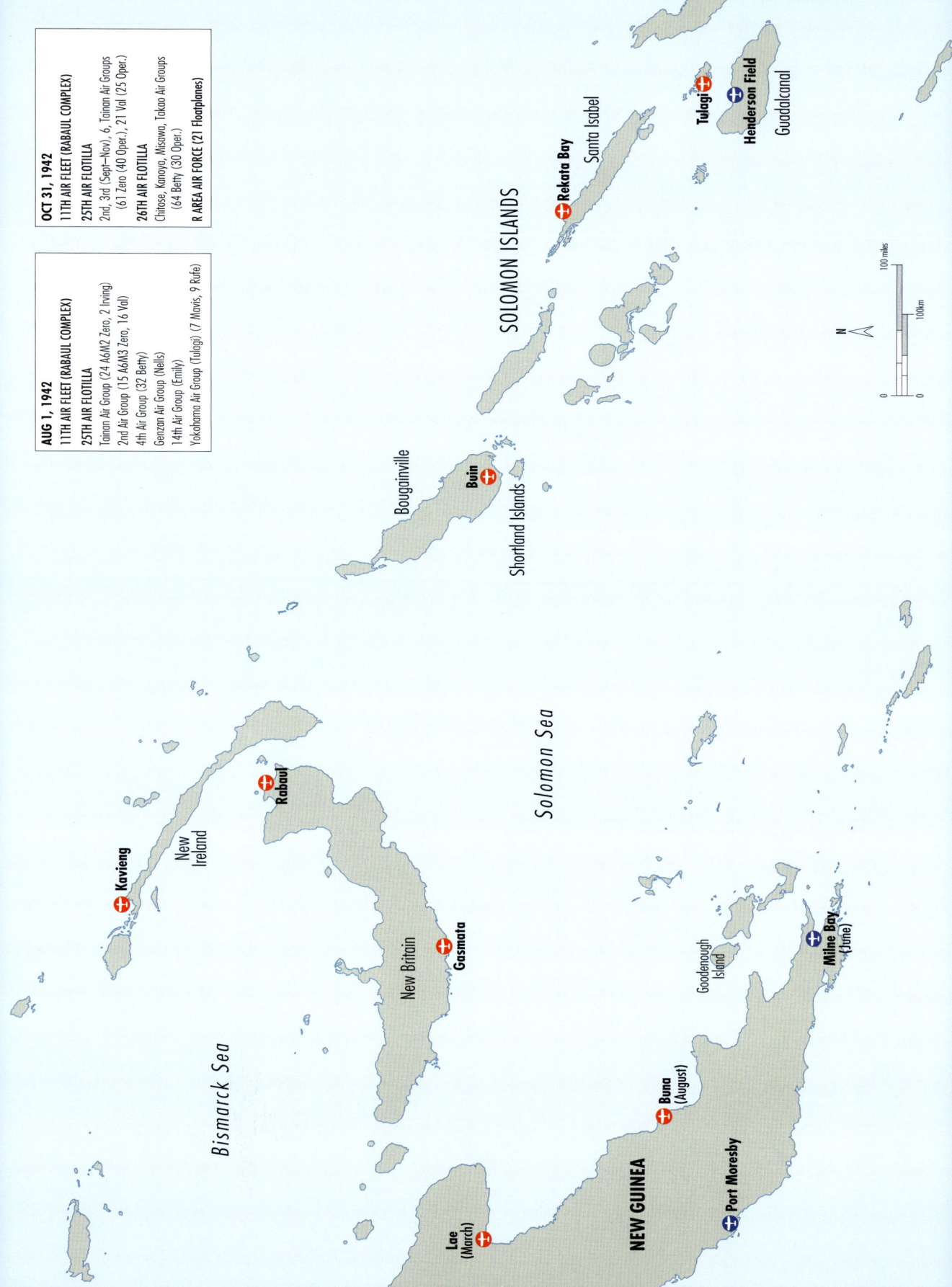

OPPOSITE JAPAN'S SOUTH PACIFIC AIR WAR

operations over water. However, the necessity of gaining air superiority over New Guinea and the Solomons was undeniable, and by late October the Army General Staff had decided to send IJAAF assets to the region. Accordingly, on November 18, the Imperial Army and Navy reached an agreement which included the commitment of the IJA's 6th Air Division (formed on November 25, 1942, under the command of Lieutenant General Itahana Giichi) to the South Pacific. This was followed by an agreement on January 3, 1943, which delineated the areas of responsibility for IJAAF and IJNAF units. Army air units were tasked to support the ground forces on New Guinea and for supporting the movement of men and supplies to New Guinea. Naval air units were responsible for conducting air operations in the Solomons and for air operations in New Guinea not assigned to the IJA. While this division of responsibility was not always adhered to, it did provide the operational framework for the rest of the air war in the South Pacific.

Between December 1942 and April 1943, the principal IJAAF aircraft conducting operations over New Guinea was the "Oscar." Like the IJN, the IJA prized maneuverability in its fighters. In December 1937, design work began on a new fighter to replace the Nakajima Ki-27. Early designs of the new Ki-43 failed to match the Ki-27's maneuverability, but the new fighter did possess a longer range. Once a Fowler flap was added to the new design, it surpassed the Ki-27 in maneuverability. Though blessed with good range and great maneuverability, it possessed a mediocre top speed, 268 knots, and was inadequately armed with a mix of cowl-mounted 7.7mm or 12.7mm machine guns. Despite its weak armament and lack of protection for the pilot and fuel tank, the Oscar acquired a good reputation against Allied forces early in the war. It looked much like the Zero, so was often confused by Allied aviators for its IJNAF cousin.

The IJAAF Oscar joined the campaign when the 11th and 1st Regiments, considered crack units, arrived at Rabaul on December 18, 1942 and January 9, 1943, respectively. The Oscar joined the Zero in providing cover for New Guinea resupply convoys and took part in several late-campaign air battles. (Claringbould)

A small number of Kawasaki Ki-48 Army Type 99 Twin-engine Light Bomber Model 1 "Lily" aircraft reached Rabaul in December 1942. The standard IJAAF light bomber of the day, the Lily was unsuccessful. It lacked the speed to escape from enemy fighters, lacked protection for its crew and fuel tanks, and possessed a weak defensive armament of only three machine guns. Its offensive capabilities were limited to a small payload of 882lb.

The first IJAAF unit to reach the South Pacific was the 76th Independent Reconnaissance Squadron, which arrived at Rabaul on October 12 with ten Ki-46-II "Dinah" twin-engine reconnaissance aircraft. The Dinah was very successful in the reconnaissance role, as it proved difficult for Allied fighters to intercept at high altitudes. The IJNAF also flew this aircraft. This lead unit was followed by the 12th Air Brigade with the 1st and 11th Regiments. Both units were considered by the Japanese to be elite, and both had combat experience. Both began the war flying the Ki-27 fighter and performed well during the DEI campaign. The 1st Regiment converted to the Oscar between June and July 1942; the 11th Regiment followed in August and September. The 11th Regiment was the first to arrive at Rabaul on December 18, 1942, with 57 Oscars. It was immediately thrown into action to cover the January convoy to Lae. Flying 283 sorties, it claimed 15 kills for the steep price of 23 Oscars and six pilots lost. On January 9, 1943, the 1st Regiment arrived at Rabaul with 53 Oscars. Both fighter units were briefly active over Guadalcanal in late January and early February. The third IJAAF regiment to reach the South Pacific was the 45th Regiment, a unit equipped with Ki-48 Lily light bombers. With its 20 bombers, it reached Rabaul in December 1942.

Japanese air facilities

The major base complex at Rabaul, located on the Gazelle Peninsula on the northeastern tip of New Britain, directly supported operations in the Solomons and New Guinea. This prewar British possession included two well-developed airfields – a civilian facility at Lakunai and a military airfield at Vunakanau, located 9 miles south of Rabaul town. The Japanese seizure of Rabaul on January 23 encountered only brief resistance, allowing work to begin immediately to convert the naval and air facilities for Japanese use. By January 25, Lakunai was ready to receive fighters and could operate bombers the following month. Vunakanau became the primary IJNAF airfield in the Rabaul complex. In addition to the two existing airfields, after its arrival in the theater the IJAAF completed Rapopo 14 miles southeast of Rabaul town in December 1942. These airfields featured concrete runways and an extensive network of 80–120 revetments at each airfield. The number of revetments among the four airfields totaled 265 for fighters and 166 for bombers. These facilities were subjected to persistent Allied attack during 1942 and 1943. Nevertheless, the Japanese proved very adept at keeping them operational.

Beyond the Rabaul area, the Japanese used other air bases, the most important of which was Lae on the northeast coast of New Guinea on the Huon Gulf. With its single runway, it was an important air hub before the war. On March 8, 1942, Lae was seized by the Japanese. Two days later, 11 Zeros from the 4th Air Group deployed there. Lae became an important staging base for IJNAF fighters and bombers. The IJAAF also used the base extensively. Other bases of note included Kavieng, located on the northern tip of New Ireland. Kavieng, which had the advantage of being out of range of most Allied aircraft, was used extensively by IJNAF fighters and bombers. Finally, Gasmata, on the south-central coast of New Britain, and Buna, on the northeast coast of New Guinea, southeast of Lae, were used by the IJNAF as staging bases for operations over New Guinea. No aircraft were permanently based at either location.

OPPOSITE
Air Vice-Marshal William Bostock, left, and Lieutenant General George Brett were the chief of staff and commander, respectively, of Allied Air Forces between April 20 and August 4, 1942. Though their combined command worked adequately, process and personnel difficulties dogged their organization, and Brett's performance displeased MacArthur. Bostock became head of RAAF Command in September. (Claringbould)

DEFENDER'S CAPABILITIES
Operational issues

Though Allied air capabilities improved significantly during 1942, the campaign opened with the Allies at a decided disadvantage. The US and Australia were forced to improvise complementary organizational and command structures to effectively employ their limited air resources. Prewar Australian government funding had been woefully inadequate, which, coupled with Australian support for Britain, left the Royal Australian Air Force (RAAF) with few combat-worthy aircraft and experienced pilots on hand. Furthermore, the agreement between the US and Britain to concentrate on defeating Germany meant that the Pacific theater would receive only enough American equipment and manpower to hold Japan in check until victory was achieved in Europe.

The Kittyhawk first saw action with No 75 Squadron in March 1942 and remained the RAAF's front-line fighter throughout the campaign. Though it could not compete with the Zero in a turning dogfight, it managed to hold its own when flown with appropriate tactics. This is a No 75 Squadron Kittyhawk. (Claringbould)

Command organization and leadership

It was well into 1942 before the Allies put in place an effective command structure staffed with the right leaders to best employ their increasing assets. After the US retreated from the Philippines to Australia, MacArthur had to quickly establish his new headquarters and mesh it with the Australian command structure already in place. On the air side, this was a challenging task since the RAAF was divided within itself on how to participate in combined operations. Disputes and jealousies among senior Australian officials and RAAF personnel resulted in an arrangement in

which RAAF headquarters retained responsibility for manning, training, and equipping the RAAF but not for air operations.

On February 23, Major General George H. Brett was made commander of United States Army Forces in Australia (USAFIA) in Brisbane. He planned to base USAAF units at Darwin, Townsville, Brisbane, Sydney, Melbourne, Adelaide, and Perth. On April 20, Brett, promoted to lieutenant general, assumed command of the new Allied Air Forces Headquarters in Melbourne. All US units, remaining Dutch air units, and RAAF combat units were assigned to the new headquarters. RAAF headquarters, headed by Air Vice-Marshal George Jones, retained administrative control over all RAAF units. Brett's staff had both US and Australian officers, including Air Vice-Marshal William Bostock as Brett's chief of staff. Due to the greater number of RAAF officers on hand, USAAF operations were greatly influenced by RAAF procedures. Brett's staff used the Australian directorate system, which allowed directors to issue orders in the commander's name.

Though this arrangement sometimes led to confusion in the field, it was initially retained when Major General George Kenney replaced Brett on August 4. MacArthur, unhappy with the performance of Allied air units under Brett, laid out for Kenney areas he felt needed improvement. Kenney, whose background included time as an instructor at the US Army Air Corps Tactical School, where he developed doctrine and tactics for interdiction operations and oversight of aircraft technical matters while on the Air Corps staff, was ideally suited to employ the limited means available to achieve MacArthur's objectives.

Activation of the USAAF 5th Air Force on September 3 and Kenney's assumption of command meant the reversion to separate USAAF and RAAF operational command structures and staffs, under the overall command of Kenney as Allied Air Forces commander. The operational RAAF Command under the Allied Air Forces was held by Bostock, who had interwar experience on the Royal Air Force Bomber Command staff and had also served as RAAF Deputy Chief of Staff with responsibility for operations and intelligence. Jones remained RAAF Chief of Staff.

Seeking to correct operational deficiencies he identified during a familiarization visit to Port Moresby, Kenney posted Brigadier General Ennis Whitehead there as commander of the 5th Air Force Advanced Echelon (ADVON) to direct New Guinea air operations. In this doctrinally unorthodox structure, Whitehead aggressively played a vital role in defending New Guinea throughout the rest of the campaign. Kenney also appointed Lieutenant Colonel (later Brigadier General) Paul Wurtsmith head of V Fighter Command and Brigadier General Kenneth Walker head of V Bomber Command to bring greater vigor to operations. After Walker was killed in action over Rabaul on January 5, 1943, Brigadier General Howard K. Ramey assumed command. When Ramey was then lost on a March 26 reconnaissance mission, Kenney temporarily retained the position himself until choosing Colonel Roger Ramey of the 43rd Bomb Group for command on April 16.

On the RAAF side, Group Captain William "Bull" Garing became commander of No 9 Operational Group responsible for New Guinea operations. He was a capable, energetic officer who complimented the American leadership. No 9 Operational Group was formed on September 1 from all RAAF combat units previously controlled by the RAAF Northeastern Area Headquarters at Townsville. It came under the operational control of Allied Air Forces, control being practically exercised by Whitehead as ADVON. On February 14, 1943, Garing was succeeded as Commander of No 9 Group by Air Commodore J. E. Hewitt, an equally capable officer who previously served as Kenney's Director for Intelligence at Allied Air Forces Headquarters.

Generals George Kenney, right, and Ennis Whitehead took over command and deputy command, respectively, when 5th Air Force was activated on September 3. They were like-minded leaders committed to implementing innovative ideas to get the most effective results out of modest Allied air resources. (NARA)

Allied aircraft

Allied airpower was initially lacking in both quantity and quality. As the Japanese air campaign got underway, the RAAF could muster only five squadrons for the immediate defense of New Guinea. In March, these were No 32 Squadron, equipped with Lockheed A-29A Hudson light bomber/reconnaissance aircraft, Nos 11 and 20 Squadrons with Consolidated PBY-5 Catalina patrol aircraft/bombers, No 24 Squadron with Commonwealth Aircraft Corporation CAC-3 Wirraway fighters/light attack aircraft, and No 75 Squadron with Curtiss P-40E Kittyhawk fighters.

Flown with appropriate tactics, the Kittyhawk could contend with the Zero. It had a range of 650 miles and a maximum speed of 354 knots at 15,000ft. Armed with six .50-caliber machine guns, it packed a heavy punch and was solidly built and armored to withstand battle damage. While a creditable strafer, the Kittyhawk lacked the maneuverability of the Zero, so was ill-suited to engage the Japanese fighter in a dogfight.

The Wirraway, an Australian modification of the US North American NA-16 trainer, performed as a dive-bomber/light attack aircraft in RAAF service after failing as a pure fighter. It carried two fixed, forward-firing .30-caliber machine guns, one swivel-mounted .30-caliber machine gun for the observer, a bomb load of 500–1,000lb, and had a 720-mile range. The Hudson carried a 1,600lb bomb load up to 1,550 miles and mounted four .30-caliber machine guns (two in the nose and two in a dorsal turret). With a range of 2,545 miles and a bomb load up to 4,000lb, the Catalina was able to reach any target in the theater, but its relatively slow speed made it vulnerable to antiaircraft fire and Japanese fighters in daylight, despite its defensive armament of seven .30-caliber machine guns.

Later, two additional RAAF Kittyhawk squadrons joined the campaign, No 76 in July 1942 and No 77 in February 1943. The RAAF also added another Wirraway squadron, No 4, and three twin-engine bomber/ground attack squadrons. These were No 22 Squadron, equipped with Douglas A-20A Boston light bombers (originally ordered by the Dutch), No 30 Squadron with Bristol Beaufighter attack aircraft, and No 100 Squadron with Bristol Beaufort torpedo bombers. The RAAF designated No 22 Squadron as an "intruder" unit, while No 30 Squadron was termed a "long-range fighter" unit. The Beaufort had a top speed of 268 knots, a range of 1,450 miles, and a payload of either one 21in. torpedo or 1,000–1,500lb of bombs, depending on whether external racks were fitted. The Boston, like the US version used in the theater, was modified to carry four .50-caliber machine

No 22 Squadron Bostons were modified like USAAF A-20As for low-altitude missions, but had initial technical problems dropping parafrag bomblets. The RAAF designated No 22 Squadron an "intruder" unit. It began operations from Five Mile 'Drome on November 15, and participated heavily in the fighting at Buna and Wau. (Claringbould)

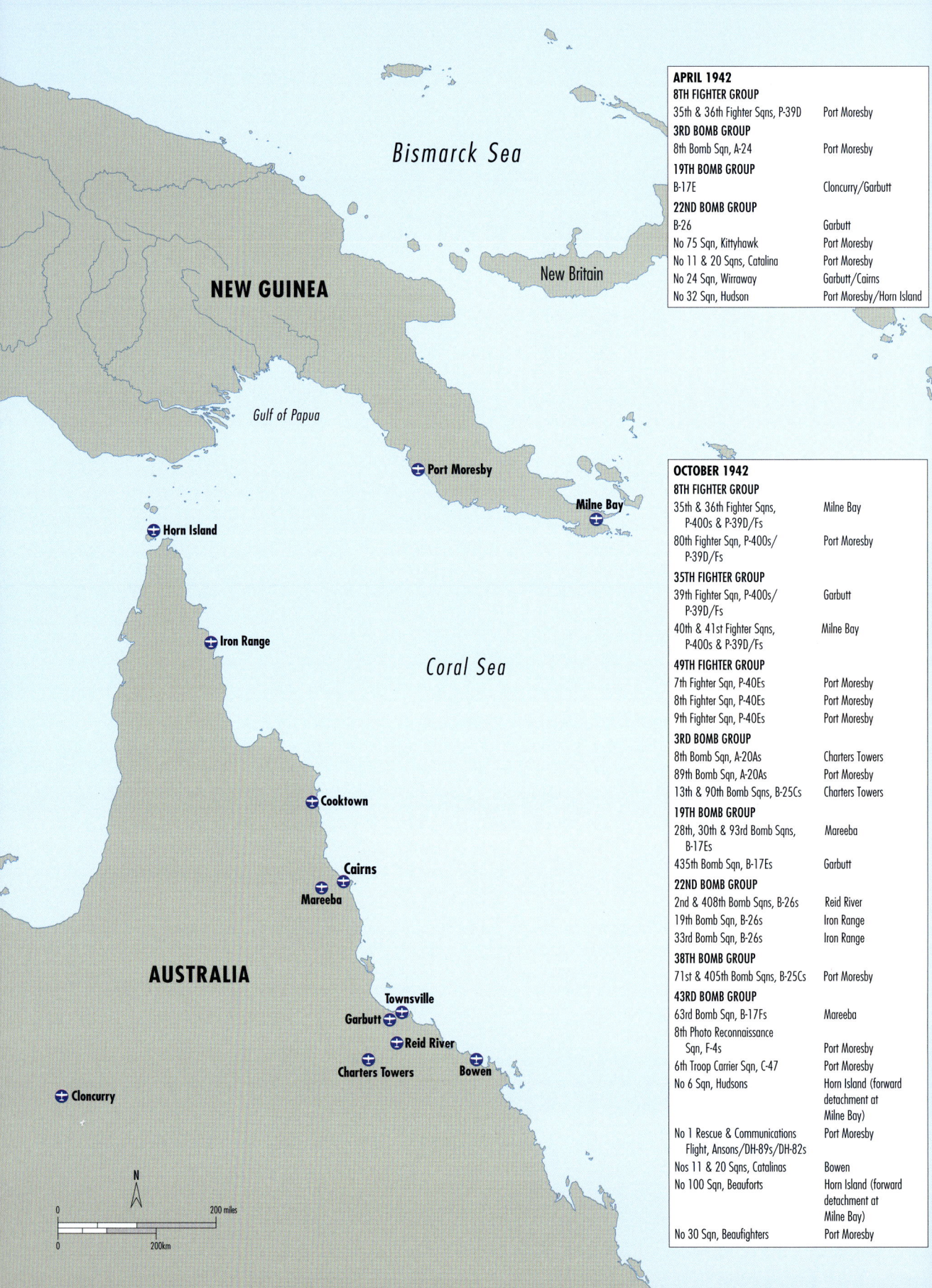

OPPOSITE THE GROWTH OF ALLIED AIRPOWER

No 30 Squadron Beaufighters provided the Allies with significant punch in low-altitude attacks against land and maritime targets. The RAAF termed it a "long-range fighter". It was armed with four 20mm nose cannon and six .30-caliber machine guns in its wings, and had a range of 1,400 miles. (Claringbould)

guns in the nose, in addition to two fuselage-mounted .30-caliber machine guns along with three .50-caliber machine guns for self-defense. Either conventional or parafrag bombs (23lb fragmentation bombs with parachutes and instantaneous fuses) could be carried. It had a top speed of over 300 knots and a range of 1,025 miles with a 2,000lb bomb load. The Beaufighter carried four 20mm cannon in the nose and six .30-caliber machine guns in the wings, had a top speed of 320 knots, and a range of 1,400 miles. All three aircraft were well-suited to ground attack as well as low-level maritime strike missions.

The USAAF situation as the campaign began was similarly gloomy. Despite respectable numbers of both bombers and fighters having been sent to Australia since December 1941, by March 1942 only about half of them were operational. Available bombers included the Boeing B-17D/E and the Consolidated B-24D and LB-30 (export version of the B-24A, diverted from RAF service) heavy bombers of the 19th Bomb Group, Douglas A-24A/B dive-bombers (Army version of the Navy's SBD Dauntless) of the 3rd Bomb Group, the 3rd Bomb Group's North American B-25Cs and the 22nd Bomb Group's Martin B-26A medium bombers, and the 3rd Bomb Group's Douglas A-20A light bombers. In November, the 90th Bomb Group's B-24Ds joined operations. However, of these, only the B-17s and A-24s were immediately available in any numbers. The B-17 and B-24/LB-30 each carried a crew of ten, had top speeds of just under 300 knots, ranges of around 2,000 miles, and carried multiple .50- and .30-caliber machine guns for defense, in addition to up to 6,000lb of bombs. Since the LB-30 lacked superchargers for its four Pratt and Whitney engines, its service ceiling was limited to about 12,000ft, well under half that of the B-17 and B-24, but by mid-1942 three aircraft had been fitted with air-to-surface radar and transitioned to the reconnaissance role. The A-24 had a maximum bomb load of 2,250lb, assuming the use of underwing racks, but its limited range of around 700–800 miles meant it could only reach targets in and around southeastern New Guinea; its limited effectiveness led to the type's withdrawal from combat in late July.

The twin-engine bombers possessed generally good performance characteristics. In addition to the A-20's performance details provided above, USAAF A-20s had their fuselage-mounted .30-caliber machine guns replaced with .50-caliber weapons. Both the B-25 and B-26 combined adequate defensive armament with top speeds just under 290 knots and ranges of

A 3rd Bomb Group 89th Bomb Squadron A-20A converted for low-altitude attack. The 89th's personnel endured delays in Australia for six months, first waiting to receive their aircraft, then for modifications to carry four nose-mounted .50-caliber guns and the 23lb "parafrag" bomblets the unit introduced in combat on August 31. (Claringbould)

1,350 miles and 1,100 miles, respectively. However, each aircraft normally carried only about half (2,000–3,000lb) of their rated maximum bomb loads due to the need to ensure adequate fuel to contend with New Guinea's difficult terrain and weather conditions. Later in the campaign, B-25s of the 3rd Bomb Group's 90th Squadron were converted from level bombers to "commerce destroyers" with the installation of four .50-caliber machine guns in the nose that, in addition to two more on either side of the fuselage and the two in the top turret facing forward, provided an awesome punch for low-level attacks. Correspondingly, the tail and belly turrets were removed.

Allied fighters possessed inferior performance to the Zero. The 49th Fighter Group's Curtiss P-40E and 8th and 35th Fighter Groups' Bell P-39D and P-400 were available by April. The P-39D/P-400 possessed superior low-altitude speed, but its un-supercharged Allison engine severely limited its performance above 12,000ft. Armed with two cowl-mounted .50-caliber machine guns, four .30-caliber machine guns in the wings, and either a 37mm (P-39) or 20mm (P-400) cannon firing through the propeller hub, it had adequate firepower, though the three different calibers complicated both aerial gunnery (all had different trajectories) and logistics. Progressive minor upgrades to the P-39 during the campaign did not remedy its basic air-to-air combat weaknesses. Its range of about 650 miles was adequate for most intercept and escort duties, and, like the P-40E, it could extend its range using a belly tank.

When the 35th Fighter Group received the P-38F in late 1942, the fighter performance balance began to shift more in the Allies' favor. Though much larger and heavier than the Zero and the Oscar, the P-38F had adequate maneuverability and excellent higher-altitude performance. Its turbocharged Allison engines delivered a top speed of 414 knots, though performance decreased once the fighter dropped to around 10,000–15,000ft. Firepower consisted of four .50-caliber machine guns and one 20mm cannon in the nose. Its short range of 650 miles was a matter of concern, with locally manufactured drop tanks being ordered to address the problem. Also on strength was the F-4A, the photo reconnaissance variant of the P-38F, having begun operations with the 8th Photo Reconnaissance Squadron in April.

The P-38F became operational only after several early mechanical problems were corrected. It entered service with the 35th Fighter Group's 39th Fighter Squadron. Though larger and heavier than other fighters, its twin turbocharged Allison engines gave American pilots more tactical options than with the P-39 or P-40 against Japanese fighters. (Claringbould)

A limited number of Lockheed C-47 transport aircraft were available throughout the campaign, though airborne transport needs were often met by a varied assortment of RAAF aircraft along with co-opted Australian civilian aircraft. Even B-17s and LB-30s were occasionally employed to carry troops and supplies. The C-47 was initially employed for cargo transport, but was later also used for troop transport/resupply drops. The C-47 could carry 6,000lb of cargo, 28 troops, or 18 stretchers for medical evacuation. Racks for up to six parachute pack containers could be mounted under the fuselage. On November 12, 1942, the 374th Troop Carrier Group was formed to include all 5th Air Force C-47s.

Allied air facilities

The Allied response to the Japanese offensive was initially blunted by the long distances of key targets from the limited bases available and the primitive condition of those bases. Air bases in Australia, while comparatively well-appointed, were few and widely scattered over its vast territory. Some Japanese targets were on New Britain and thus beyond the reach of most Allied combat aircraft based in Australia. Bombers therefore had to stage from Australian bases such as Townsville to Port Moresby or Milne Bay the day prior to flying missions against New Britain. Airfields on New Guinea ("dromes" in RAAF parlance) were in most cases simply areas cleared out of the jungle, with frequent rain turning runways and taxiways into quagmires until proper surfacing and drainage was completed. Even with the use of American perforated steel plank (PSP, or Marston mats) placed on runways to provide stability and traction, operations at these airfields were often quite difficult. In almost all cases, proper maintenance shelters, dispersal hardstands, or protective revetments were lacking, and serviceability of Allied aircraft remained a limiting factor throughout the campaign. Personnel lived and worked in tents or shelters made from crude lumber and jungle growth; to avoid air attack, they dove into waterlogged slit trenches. Crews staging to Port Moresby often slept under their aircraft's wings.

Throughout the campaign, air defense of New Guinea airfields was generally limited to machine guns due to a shortage of heavier antiaircraft artillery. Seven Mile 'Drome at Port Moresby had a few 37mm guns during the initial fighter deployment by No 75 Squadron in March 1942. Later, the US deployed the 745th Antiaircraft Battalion with 16 90mm guns to Port Moresby, but exactly how many of these were deployed at the surrounding airfields is unclear. A battery of the Australian 2/3rd Light Antiaircraft Regiment also deployed Bofors 40mm L/60 automatic guns by May. Milne Bay also had a battery from the 2/3rd and the US 104th Antiaircraft Battalion by July, both with 40mm Bofors, and received the US 709th Antiaircraft Machine Gun Battery on August 24, just before the Japanese assault.

An 8th Fighter Group P-39D, probably of the 35th Fighter Squadron, undergoes maintenance at Milne Bay, where the 35th and 36th Fighter Squadrons relieved Nos 75 and 76 Squadrons on September 21. Maintenance in New Guinea's primitive, rainy conditions was challenging, and Allied operational rates rarely rose above 50 percent. (MacArthur Memorial)

CAMPAIGN OBJECTIVES
Extending the perimeter

Japanese plans and objectives

The Kawanishi H6K Navy Type 97 Flying Boat "Mavis" was used by the IJNAF for bombing, reconnaissance, and transport. It carried up to 2,205lb of bombs and had a range of 4,210 miles. The Yokohama Air Group's Mavises launched the opening strike of the campaign against Port Moresby on February 3, 1942. (Author's Collection)

Japan's goal in the South Pacific was to extend its defensive perimeter to resist future Allied attempts to reverse Japan's conquests in the DEI and Southeast Asia as key parts of its Greater East Asia Co-Prosperity Sphere. The IGHQ directed in late January 1942 that the IJA's South Seas Force and IJN's 4th Fleet cooperate to seize key locations on New Guinea to neutralize Australia by severing communication between it and the US.

The Japanese conducted multiple operations between March and August to implement this strategy. The initial Japanese move against New Guinea, Operation *SR*, was executed on March 8 by South Seas Force troops in landings at Salamaua on Huon Bay along the north Papuan coast and the seizure of Lae by Special Naval Landing Forces (SNLF) to the north. This was followed by Operation *MO*, the dispatch from Rabaul on May 4 of a convoy carrying troops to invade Port Moresby after a planned landing at nearby Taurama Beach on May 10. The convoy never arrived, having been turned back at the battle of the Coral Sea. Another outgrowth of the failed Port Moresby invasion was the Japanese occupation of Tulagi in the southern Solomons on May 3. Nearby Guadalcanal was occupied the following month and construction of an airfield begun there, leading to an American counterattack to seize the airfield before it could be finished. This was the start of the prolonged struggle for Guadalcanal, which ran from early August until early February 1943. In early June, Japan launched an attack against the Aleutians and a thrust toward Midway Atoll. The Aleutian operation met with initial success, and the islands of Attu and Kiska were secured by June 7. However, the Imperial Navy suffered a major defeat on June 4 at the battle of Midway, losing four carriers.

The Coral Sea and Midway defeats caused the IGHQ to reevaluate its priorities. Lacking adequate carrier-borne air support after these battles, Japan's focus swung to the South Pacific, where land-based airpower could support offensive operations, assuming Japan secured enough air bases from which to operate. A renewed assault on Port Moresby was to be made overland, dubbed Operation *RE*. On July 21, the South Sea Force's Yokoyama Advance Force, comprising about 1,800 troops and 1,300 support personnel, landed at Buna on Papua's northeast coast. This force pushed inland along the Kokoda Trail, the only path from Buna through the jungles and over the Owen Stanley Range that significant ground forces could possibly traverse toward Port Moresby. On July 29, Japanese forces seized Kokoda, and by August 13 they had captured and halted at Isurava, roughly 40 miles from Buna. With the arrival of an additional 8,450 IJA South Seas Force troops, the overland push to Port Moresby resumed on August 26. However, the Japanese drive halted at Ioribaiwa on September 17 – only some 30 miles from its objective. This was due to major difficulties the Japanese had in adequately supplying their forces over the difficult Kokoda Trail route, the failure of the Milne Bay assault, and orders to await the outcome of the ongoing Guadalcanal effort.

The Japanese planned to support the South Seas Force move toward Port Moresby via the Kokoda Trail by the seizure of Australian positions around Milne Bay in extreme eastern Papua. Once this area, with two completed airfields and another under construction, was secured, the Japanese aimed to advance along the southeastern coast toward Port Moresby, supplying their troops by barges, in a pincer movement coordinated with a renewed push south along the Kokoda Trail. Japan also planned to use forces stationed at Milne Bay to solidify control over the Coral Sea approaches to Australia and launch future operations against the archipelagoes further southeast.

The Japanese assaulted the north shore of Milne Bay on August 26 with some 1,500 SNLF troops. However, the previously meager Allied ground and air presence had been reinforced shortly before the attack and the Japanese landing was defeated within a week, the first time Japanese ground forces had been beaten in the war. At the same time, the Japanese were finding it more difficult to supply their forces along the Kokoda Trail and at Buna, so were forced to await an Allied counterattack. This came on September 26; after bitter fighting, the Japanese were forced back over the Owen Stanleys by a combined American–Australian offensive along the Kokoda Trail. The Allied offensive was renewed in October when US and Australian ground force elements were airlifted to Wanigela and began to push west, in concert with the US 32nd Infantry Division and the 7th Australian Brigade pushing northeast against Japan's Buna–Sanananda–Gona position. After three months of bitter fighting, starving and outnumbered Japanese troops ceased all resistance on January 22, 1943.

Zeros, probably of the Tainan Air Group, take off from Lae in mid-1942. Both the IJNAF and IJAAF used Lae for deployments of fighters, bombers, and reconnaissance aircraft. It was a constant threat to the Allies because of its proximity to Port Moresby, and the Allies accordingly attacked it regularly. (Claringbould)

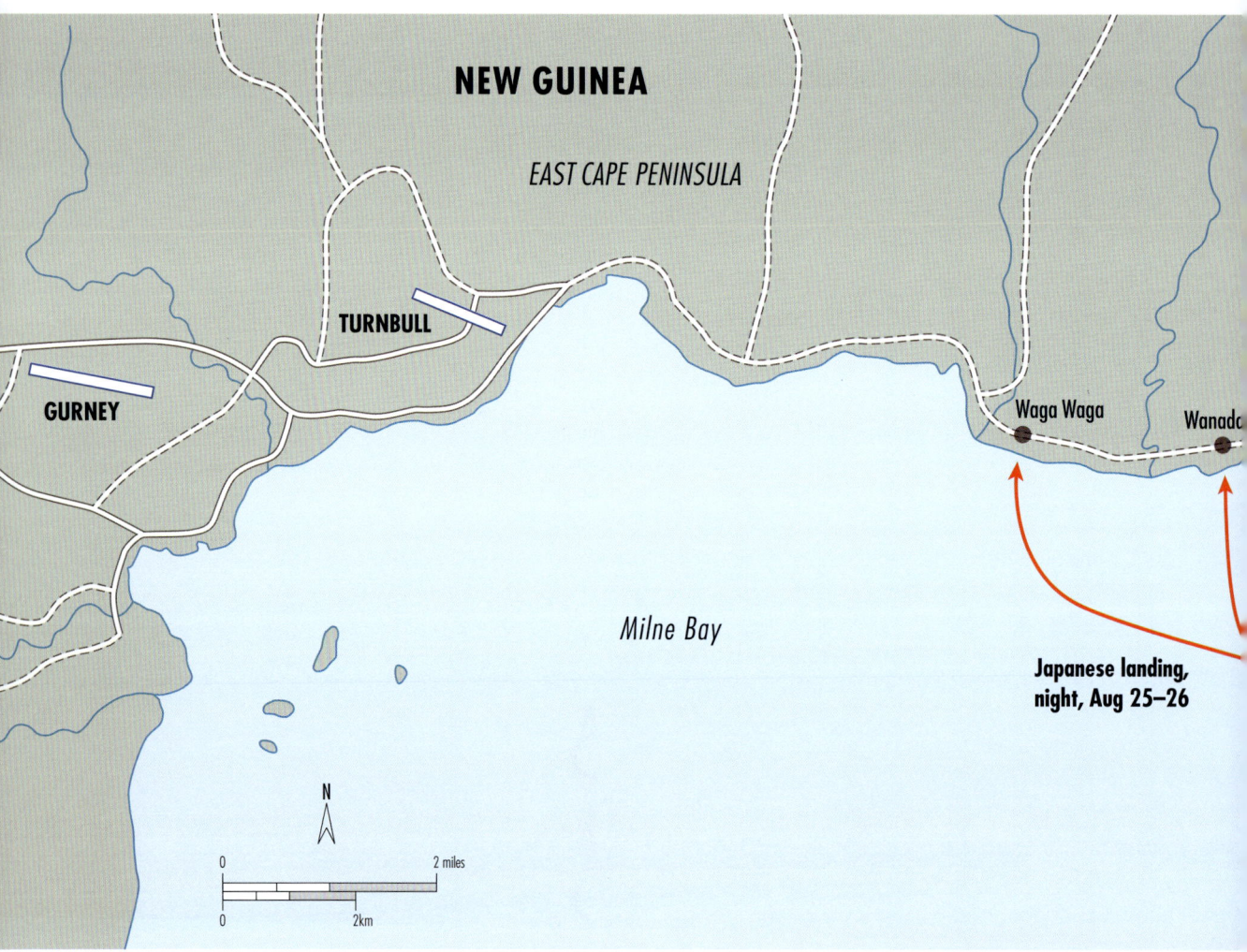

The loss of Buna emphasized Japan's need to protect its remaining positions in New Guinea, particularly those around the Huon Gulf seized the previous March at Lae and Salamaua. Correspondingly, the IGHQ decided to maintain an "active defense" holding action in the Solomons while redoubling its offensive efforts in New Guinea. Japan seized locations for major rear-area bases on the northern coast further west at Wewak and Madang on December 18. On January 27, 1943, elements of the Japanese 18th Army attacked Wau, a gold mining site southwest of Lae and Salamaua that had remained in the hands of the Australian Kanga Force throughout 1942. However, the Australians stopped the Japanese by January 30 due to timely reinforcements delivered by air, and by early April Australian troops had stabilized the front just short of Salamaua and were awaiting an Allied buildup to attack Japan's Huon Gulf positions. In addition to making the overland attack against the Australians at Wau, the Japanese renewed attempts to resupply and reinforce the Huon Gulf garrisons from Rabaul in March and to destroy Allied forces at Port Moresby and Milne Bay by air attacks during *I-Go* in April. The failure of all these efforts put the Japanese on the strategic defensive in New Guinea from April 1943 onwards.

OPPOSITE OPERATION *RE*

Allied plans and objectives

The initial Allied reaction to Japan's takeover of the DEI and Philippines was to prepare for a defense of Australia itself. The Australian Chiefs of Staff briefed MacArthur on a plan to cede much of northern and western Australia to the Japanese while defending a line running diagonally from Brisbane to Adelaide. Early on, MacArthur rejected this so-called "Brisbane Line" and determined to hold the Japanese at New Guinea so that ultimately the Allies could turn defense into offense without sacrificing any Australian territory. Though Allied forces were weak, he believed the location and topography of New Guinea, particularly the barrier formed by the Owen Stanley Range, offered the Allies a chance to stymie the Japanese while building up forces for a counterpunch. A request made by MacArthur in May for additional aircraft (500-plus), ground troops (three divisions), and naval forces (two British carriers) was rejected by the Joint Chiefs. This left MacArthur with very limited resources, particularly in airborne and seaborne transport, with which to hold New Guinea.

The Allies began to build up bases in northeastern Australia to handle whatever American troops, aircraft, and supplies could be expected as part of the overall "hold the line in the Pacific while pushing for victory in Europe" strategy. The battle of the Coral Sea provided the Allies with a bit of breathing space to improve their position on New Guinea. The Allies used this respite to make improvements to facilities and for the building of airfields at Port Moresby and Milne Bay, while deploying additional troops to both locations and to Wau in the Bulolo Valley southwest of Lae. Allied plans made in mid-July to occupy Buna on the northeast coast and improve the airfield at Dobodura, however, were not executed rapidly enough, and the Japanese landing at Buna on July 21 forced MacArthur to reassess his options.

MacArthur's staff had formulated a plan to seize Buna and intensify the Allied assault on Rabaul from New Guinea in conjunction with a potential Allied push up the Solomons toward New Ireland. But with Buna in Japanese hands and their troops pressing down the Kokoda Trail toward Port Moresby, the Allies had to revise plans from a less tactically tenable position. MacArthur devised a three-pronged strategy to assault Buna and eliminate the Japanese from the northeast coast. This plan envisioned a thrust along the Kokoda Trail, a push north along the Kapa–Jaure track by an Allied column further to the east, and airborne delivery of Allied troops to a new airstrip at Wanigela and their movement along the northern coast to secure Cape Nelson and thereafter participate in the assault on Buna.

After the September destruction of the Japanese beachhead at Milne Bay and the success in halting the Japanese attack along the Kokoda Trail 30 miles short of Port Moresby, MacArthur was in a position to execute this plan. The direct Allied push up the Kokoda Trail began on September 26. By mid-November, the remaining Allied forces, having moved overland and by air, were in position on the northern side of the Owen Stanley Range. In a related operation in late October, the Australians cleared Goodenough Island of part of a Japanese force stranded there heading for Milne Bay in August. This eliminated potential attacks against the planned coastal barge operation from Milne Bay that was needed to keep Allied forces on the coastal axis of advance against Buna supplied. On November 19, the Allied assault on the Japanese positions began. Extremely hard fighting by Allied ground forces, coupled with the denial of adequate supplies and reinforcements to the Japanese garrison, resulted in the total collapse of the Japanese at the Buna–Sanananda–Gona defense complex by January 22, 1943. This put the Allies into position to go on the offensive later in the year.

THE CAMPAIGN
Putting the pressure on

Punch-counterpunch – New Guinea and New Britain

Almost immediately after the Japanese occupied Rabaul and as they were still consolidating their position on the rest of New Britain, they initiated action to neutralize Port Moresby. The IJNAF's 24th Air Flotilla, having received additional forces, created the 4th Air Group at Rabaul's airfields on February 10. The 4th's authorized strength from February to April 1942 was 36 A6M2 Zeros and 36 Bettys, though it initially had on hand only 12 and nine, respectively. Also subordinate to the 24th was the Yokohama Air Group, with eight of 18 authorized "Mavis" long-range flying boats. Initially, the 4th also operated 27 obsolescent A5M Claude fighters until it received its full complement of Zeros. The 24th was also assigned the 21st Air Flotilla's 1st Air Group, with 18 G3M Nell bombers, on February 23.

On January 24 and 28, Yokohama Air Group Mavises reconnoitered Port Moresby and found very little in the way of defenses. The first bombing raid on Port Moresby town and facilities, in the early hours of February 3, was conducted by eight Mavises from about 12,000ft. Five Mavises bombed again in the early darkness on February 5; neither raid resulted in significant military damage. Warning of these raids had been provided by Australian coast watchers at Gasmata, who were captured when the Japanese seized the airfield on February 9.

There was a lull until February 24, when the IJNAF staged its first daylight raid on Port Moresby in preparation for Operation *SR*, the seizure of Salamaua and Lae. Nine Nells escorted by three Zeros attacked Seven Mile 'Drome at about noon with 132lb "daisy cutter" bombs from 20,000ft, destroying a Hudson, airfield structures, and several vehicles. On February 28, 17 Nells returned, escorted by six Zeros. Though the bombing failed to do any appreciable damage, the fighters descended to strafe Catalinas moored in Fairfax Harbor.

Beginning in early August, the IJNAF bolstered the 11th Air Fleet with "Val" dive-bombers such as this D3A2. Pulled from different air groups to add striking power, they operated from both Rabaul and Lae. The 11th Air Fleet sent them against Milne Bay, Port Moresby, and Buna-area targets. (Author's Collection)

OPPOSITE ALLIED AIRFIELDS

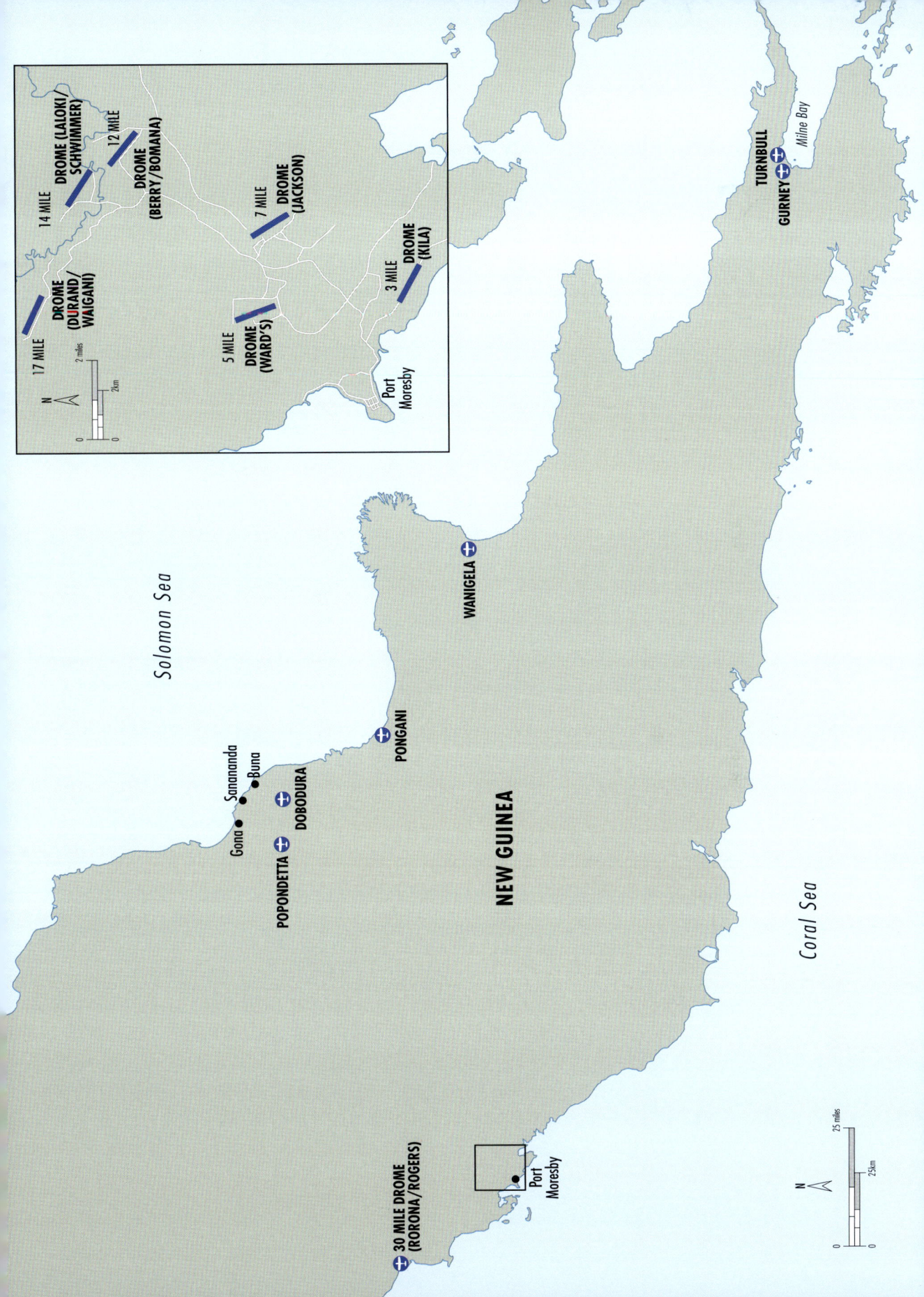

The RAAF Hudson provided yeoman service during the campaign as a bomber and, more frequently, flying invaluable reconnaissance and transport missions. It served during the campaign with Nos 6 and 32 Squadrons, early on operating from Horn Island in Australia but later at Port Moresby and Milne Bay. (Claringbould)

Three Catalinas were destroyed, but at the cost of one Zero downed by antiaircraft fire when it flew on to strafe Seven Mile 'Drome. The IJNAF did not attempt another major raid on Port Moresby until March 14.

Allied raids on Rabaul commenced immediately after its capture by the Japanese on January 24 and occurred every second night until February 3. These raids were carried out by RAAF Catalinas, which bombed ships in Simpson Harbor. After its capture, raids were also mounted against Gasmata, to which the Japanese planned to disperse fighters for defense-in-depth of Rabaul. The first Allied raid on Gasmata came during the early hours of February 10, when four Hudsons of a RAAF composite squadron (designated No 32 Squadron on February 21) fought through bad weather to perform "diving" attacks with unknown results. Later that afternoon, four more Hudsons attacked, followed by three Catalinas that night, without hitting anything. On February 11, the Japanese mounted a defense when three Hudsons conducted a mast-level attack on two troop transports in Gasmata Harbor at midday. Four Claudes, just deployed to Gasmata from Rabaul, intercepted them. The Japanese shot down two Hudsons for no loss. One Hudson crew was lost and the other was ultimately rescued, in exchange for scoring one 250lb bomb hit on *Kinryu Maru*, killing 12 and wounding 32. In the following days, IJNAF fighters chased Hudson reconnaissance missions over Rabaul and other locations on New Britain, who fought them off without loss and monitored the buildup of Japanese ships and aircraft at Rabaul. This set the stage for the first combined USAAF/RAAF attack – also the first Allied daylight raid – on Rabaul, which was originally to have been made in conjunction with a raid by aircraft from the carrier *Lexington*. However, when Japanese search aircraft discovered the carrier before it got within range of Rabaul, the US Navy cancelled its participation.

The arrival in Australia of 12 B-17D/Es by February 20 was the first substantive USAAF contribution to the New Guinea air campaign and was expected to provide greater punch against Rabaul. The Flying Fortresses wasted no time getting into action. Early on February 23, the 14th Bomb Squadron launched seven B-17Es from their Cloncurry dispersal base, but due to ferocious weather and mechanical problems, only five made it to Rabaul just after dawn. Two of the B-17Es had senior RAAF Catalina pilots aboard to provide navigation and targeting support against ships and Lakunai airfield. Only three B-17Es bombed from about 23,000ft; the other two could not locate a target and did not drop their ordnance. Bombing was inaccurate due to thick clouds obscuring the target area, despite multiple bomb runs by at least one B-17E. Six 4th Air Group Zeros and two Claudes from Lakunai

The first American participant in the campaign was the B-17E. With superior range, bomb load, and defensive firepower, it was a rugged, formidable aircraft that the Japanese struggled to shoot down. However, relatively few were available at any given time. This B-17E served with both the 19th and 43rd Bomb Groups. (Claringbould)

intercepted and managed to damage three B-17Es, one of which later ran out of fuel and crash-landed about 60 miles southeast of Buna; the crew was recovered 36 days later. The other four B-17s landed at Port Moresby, refueled, and returned to Garbutt that afternoon. Two RAAF Catalinas also participated, but only one managed to find Rabaul and drop eight 250lb bombs at Vunakanau, with unknown results. After the battle, three Zeros landed at Gasmata for a three-day deployment to conduct patrols. The Allies closed out the month with a "maximum effort" by five No 32 Squadron Hudsons on the night of February 28, flying from their Horn Island dispersal base against Gasmata. Only three aircraft bombed and claimed to have hit the airfield.

This opening round of attacks by both sides seemed to favor the Japanese. Both major base areas had proved vulnerable to bombers, though neither side had caused significant damage. However, Japanese fighters roamed at will over New Guinea, forcing Allied bombing missions to be flown at night or in bad weather, which greatly degraded accuracy, while the lack of Allied fighters left Port Moresby all but defenseless whenever the 24th Air Flotilla chose to raid.

Japan's foothold in New Guinea – Lae and Salamaua

The temporary lull in early March of Japanese pressure on Port Moresby was due to their invasion of New Guinea's north coast. Nells of 1st Air Group bombed Lae and Bulolo from March 5–7 to soften up the area prior to the impending landings, causing little damage beyond destroying a few commercial gold mining buildings. Operation *SR* had been slightly delayed by the presence of *Lexington* east of Rabaul on February 19 and 20 and the February 23 B-17 attack on Rabaul, but the joint invasion force of a battalion of IJA soldiers and a battalion of SNLF troops – accompanied by about 500 IJN construction personnel – made unopposed landings during the early morning of March 8 at Salamaua and Lae, respectively. The construction troops' immediate priority was to operationalize Lae airfield, and the first 4th Air Group deployment there occurred on March 11 in the form of seven Zeros and a few Bettys. In conjunction with Gasmata's airstrip, Lae multiplied IJNAF options by providing a much closer point of departure for attacks against Port Moresby, potentially

RAAF Catalinas provided the Allies with early long-range bombing capability, but also excelled at reconnaissance and air-sea rescue missions. They served with Nos 11 and 20 Squadrons. After early losses they moved from Port Moresby, first to Tulagi in the Solomons, then in May to Bowen in Australia. (Claringbould)

allowing increased sortie generation and greater loiter time over the target. In addition to serving as a forward staging base, Lae was a useful divert field for damaged aircraft or those avoiding foul weather.

Though the danger posed by a Japanese lodgment on New Guinea was apparent to the Allies, their opposition to the invasion came solely from the air. The few New Guinea Volunteer Rifles militia troops occupying the area retreated into the jungle just hours before the Japanese landings. The invasion force, covered by 4th Air Group Zeros, was detected on March 7 by RAAF reconnaissance, but the weather precluded any Allied airstrikes against the convoy as it transited to the landing area. On March 8, the Allies flew 11 Hudson and four B-17E sorties, but the invasion force remained protected by foul weather and only one Hudson bombed, damaging the transport *Yokohama Maru*. Due to required maintenance, the Allies were only able to mount a single Hudson reconnaissance sortie of the invasion force on March 9. However, the information obtained was used by the US Navy to plan a daring 104-plane strike on the invasion flotilla the following day from carriers *Yorktown* and *Lexington*, located in the Gulf of Papua 125 miles away. The 86 bombers and 18 fighters, flying through the 7,500ft Sunshine Gap in the Owen Stanley Range, struck beginning at 0922hrs and managed to sink three transports and a minesweeper, damage six other vessels, and cause 375 Japanese casualties. Zeros of the 4th Air Group, grounded at Gasmata due to bad weather, were unable to defend the invasion force, while two Nakajima E8N2 "Dave" floatplanes from the seaplane tender *Kiyokawa Maru* dueled with the attackers but were both destroyed by defensive fire after inflicting only light damage to three of *Lexington*'s Douglas TBD-1 Devastators. Later that day, eight 14th Reconnaissance Squadron B-17Es from Horn Island and three No 32 Squadron Hudsons from Port Moresby also attacked the invasion force. The B-17Es caused no damage; the Hudsons contributed to damage already sustained by *Kiyokawa Maru*, putting the tender and its remaining floatplanes out of action. A Dave was also lost to Hudson return fire. In the late afternoon, two more Hudsons successfully dropped 12 bombs from only 300ft, cratering Salamaua's airfield.

The success of the Japanese landing meant that Lae and Salamaua were now added to the Allied target list. Lae-deployed Zeros were busy over the next two days, defending their new airfield against Allied raids that resulted in little damage and no aircraft losses by either side. One reconnaissance Hudson was spotted by two patrolling Zeros near Lae on March 11, but the Zeros could not catch the Hudson as it dodged in and out of clouds. On March 12, three more Zeros deployed from Rabaul to Lae; the 4th Air Group now had about half its fighter strength operating from the primitive facility on New Guinea. That same day, five B-17Es, staging from Horn Island, attacked Lae's dock area and Salamaua's small airfield from 27,000ft; the crews claimed many hits on hangars, the airfield, and dock facilities. They also claimed one Zero of the three that attacked the B-17Es, but the 4th Air Group recorded suffering no losses.

Upping the ante – Allied fighters appear

The slugging match against each other's main bases continued during March, though neither side could muster a sustained, large-scale effort due to ongoing lack of serviceable aircraft and competing mission requirements. The IJNAF, learning that both Port Moresby and Horn Island were being used as staging bases for Allied raids against Rabaul, planned to suppress them. However, this proved impossible due to growing requirements in the Solomons, the need for wide-area reconnaissance ahead of a planned seaborne assault on Port Moresby, and the time needed to recover from heavy 24th Air Flotilla losses of two Mavises and 15 Bettys in a February 20 attack on *Lexington* east of Rabaul. The Allies also began the month in bad shape – the RAAF had only two serviceable Catalinas (removed to the relative safety of Tulagi in the Solomons, then in May to Bowen in Australia) and maybe six Hudsons, while the serviceability of the B-17Es rarely rose above five. The competing priority for the Allies to use these long-range aircraft for reconnaissance increased in March. The Americans also twice had to divert some of their barely airworthy B-17Es for several days in March for the evacuations of MacArthur and President Manuel Quezon from the Philippines.

During March, RAAF Hudsons and Catalinas flew a total of only 30 sorties against New Britain targets, with indifferent results. For example, on March 3, five Hudsons flying different routes attempted to hit Gasmata again. One aborted due to violent weather encountered over the Owen Stanleys, while two that did reach Gasmata after dark tried to hit the airfield through overcast, but with negligible results. Japanese antiaircraft gunners claimed the last two Hudsons, which attacked Gasmata Harbor shipping at low level; both crews were lost. In one of these wrecks, the Japanese found documents indicating that the Hudsons had flown their mission from Horn Island. As for the USAAF, B-17Es of the 40th Bomb Squadron of the 19th Bomb Group (redesignated from 14th Bomb Squadron on March 14) flew six mostly ineffectual missions against Rabaul between February 23 and April 1, totaling only 15 sorties. Raids on March 13 and 18 resulted in no appreciable damage. On March 20, four B-17Es staged from Seven Mile 'Drome to attack ships in Simpson Harbor from 31,000ft. The light cruiser *Yubari* was damaged before the bombers were attacked by four Zeros. Neither side lost any aircraft.

The 24th Air Flotilla, though stretched by multiple requirements for its limited number of aircraft, mounted several attacks against Port Moresby in March. The 4th Air Group received replacement Bettys in late February and their crews completed basic training by early March. On the 13th, five Zeros from Lae strafed Seven Mile 'Drome in the morning, hoping to catch Allied bombers at the field. However, the lone Hudson and four B-17Es had already departed for a fruitless run against Gasmata and Lakunai, respectively. The Zeros only destroyed a small transport aircraft and set fire to some fuel drums, but spotted one B-17E and the Hudson as they returned to land. The Hudson hid in clouds until the Zeros departed; the B-17E beat off its attackers and damaged one Zero that nonetheless made it back to Lae. Three additional Zeros deployed to Lae the same day, giving the 4th Air Group 13 fighters there. On the following day, the IJNAF launched an ambitious double strike against Allied airpower.

Acting on the intelligence obtained from the Hudson crash, eight 4th Air Group Bettys took off from Vunakanau on March 14 and rendezvoused with 12 Lae-deployed Zeros to strike Horn Island. Coast watchers on New Guinea notified Horn Island of the incoming

A Betty, unit unknown, takes off from Vunakanau. The Betty shouldered most of the weight of the 11th Air Fleet's campaign against Port Moresby and northeast Australia. However, it was rarely used in sufficient numbers, or bombed from low-enough altitudes, to inflict significant damage on its targets. (Claringbould)

raid and nine 49th Fighter Group P-40Es scrambled to intercept it. The 7th Fighter Squadron had just deployed to Horn Island on March 9 to bolster the RAAF's Northeast Area defenses. Just after noon, the Bettys dropped 78 bombs from 23,000ft, destroying one Hudson and damaging another, and hitting buildings and a fuel dump. Intercepting P-40Es made contact, and in the ensuing battle downed two Zeros – one by ramming – and damaged at least two Bettys. The 49th Fighter Group suffered three fighters damaged and one lost, the pilot being saved after bailing out. Since these four aircraft represented about 50 percent of the 49th's force, the squadron was withdrawn south the next day for refit. The same day, nine Bettys hit Port Moresby in a "surveillance" attack, attempting to catch bombers on the ground, but caused little damage. In addition to the March 14 double strike against both Port Moresby and Horn Island, the IJNAF flew uncontested attacks against Port Moresby on March 9, 10, 11, 19, and 20.

RAAF No 75 Squadron arrived at Seven Mile 'Drome with 17 Kittyhawks on March 21. It presented a new wrinkle for the IJNAF by becoming the first Allied fighter unit to engage directly in the New Guinea campaign. Initial RAAF fighter operations in defense of Port Moresby were severely constrained by lack of warning time of incoming Japanese raids and limits on the Kittyhawk's performance. Pilots of No 75 Squadron on alert rarely had as much as 20 minutes warning from aircraft start-up to interception of Japanese aircraft. This later led to standing air patrols during the most likely times for Japanese attacks, to allow the squadron's fighters to acquire an altitude advantage. Usually operating individually, pilots avoided dogfighting with the Zero if possible, while attacks against bombers were conducted from below or at the same altitude from the front quarter. Typically, RAAF pilots got off whatever quick shot at IJNAF aircraft that presented itself, then dove suddenly to avoid or shake off any Japanese fighters. Strafing attacks on Japanese airfields were always preceded by a reconnaissance flight and almost always consisted of just one low-level firing pass to minimize losses from antiaircraft fire. For their part, Japanese pilots flew as a group but were observed by Allied pilots to conduct combat as individuals rather than in a coordinated way.

On March 21, the 4th Air Group lost a reconnaissance Betty to a just-arrived No 75 Squadron Kittyhawk. The next day, nine Kittyhawks conducted an early-morning strafing attack on Lae, reaching their target a little after dawn. Five dove to strafe, destroying three parked Zeros and damaging numerous other aircraft. Meanwhile, four Kittyhawks fought two patrolling Zeros. The Japanese shot down two for no loss; one RAAF pilot was killed, and one later returned to the squadron. Two No 32 Squadron Hudsons attacked Lae less than an hour later. Their bombs splashed harmlessly offshore, but their return fire did manage to down two of three Zeros that pursued them. Lastly, two B-17Es bombed Lae from high altitude and claimed a hit on an ammunition dump.

The 24th Air Flotilla's March 23 attack included 19 Nells and three Zeros. Dividing into two formations to hit Seven Mile 'Drome and antiaircraft batteries at Port Moresby, the Japanese claimed the destruction of six small and one large aircraft, though none were actually hit. No 75 Squadron's ten serviceable Kittyhawks scrambled to intercept, but could not climb fast enough to catch the bombers. An hour later, a strafing attack by four Zeros destroyed two Kittyhawks mired on the runway and damaged a third, leaving only seven flyable Kittyhawks. The 24th lost one Zero and its pilot to antiaircraft fire while strafing. The next day, after losing an early-morning reconnaissance aircraft to a Kittyhawk, 18 Nells, with three escorting Zeros, hit Seven Mile 'Drome and nearby buildings from 20,000ft. One Nell was damaged by antiaircraft fire, while the Zeros engaged two intercepting Kittyhawks without loss to either side after a brief dogfight.

However, the 24th Air Flotilla could not sustain its momentum against Port Moresby. The 1st Air Group was withdrawn and the depleted 4th Air Group, though attacking Port Moresby four more times in March and reducing No 75 Squadron to only five serviceable Kittyhawks, could not muster the force needed to put No 75 Squadron completely out of action. The 4th's raid on the morning of March 25 saw only three Bettys escorted by four Zeros ineffectually bomb Port Moresby. Thick clouds and radio problems precluded a Kittyhawk interception. The 27th witnessed another attack on Seven Mile 'Drome. The Japanese met four Kittyhawks over the target, the Zeros engaging two while the other pair of Kittyhawks fired at the Bettys. One Betty and one Kittyhawk were lost with their crews, but the airfield was undamaged. A sweep by five Zeros early the next afternoon was met 30 miles northwest of Port Moresby by four Kittyhawks, an unusual occurrence given the normally brief warning times of Japanese raids. In the ensuing combat, the Zeros dove on the Kittyhawks from 8,000ft higher altitude, shooting down one and killing the pilot and damaging the other three for no loss to themselves. At midday on March 30, an impromptu fight developed, with Lae Zeros escorting one Vunakanau Betty to Port Moresby running into two 19th Bomb Group B-17Es returning from a strike on Lae that damaged some buildings and one aircraft there. As the B-17Es prepared to land at Seven Mile 'Drome to refuel before returning to Garbutt, the Zeros attacked and damaged one, but were themselves attacked and driven off by a lone Kittyhawk that had been patrolling above the airfield. The Betty bombed the airfield but caused no damage; an hour later, two more Vunakanau Bettys also attacked but likewise caused no damage. All the Bettys returned to base despite enduring antiaircraft fire.

Japanese ground crewmen manhandle 250kg bombs while arming Bettys at Vunakanau. The Japanese lost experienced ground crew to Allied attacks at an alarming rate during the campaign, and this, combined with primitive working conditions and limited spare parts, often negatively affected the 11th Air Fleet's operational readiness, especially at Lae. (Claringbould)

The battle of attrition intensifies

The air battle for New Guinea increased in intensity in April with the addition of forces on both sides. On April 1, the 25th Air Flotilla relieved the 24th at Rabaul. The 11th Air Fleet also shifted its headquarters from Formosa to Rabaul in April. The Tainan Air Group transferred from Bali and absorbed the 4th Air Group's fighters. Between April 7 and 11, Rabaul received 36 new Zeros by ship, bringing its fighter component to 45, along with five Mitsubishi C5M2 Babs reconnaissance planes. The personnel of the Tainan Air Group,

In mid-April 1942, the 4th Air Group's Zeros were absorbed into the newly arrived Tainan Air Group. This unit included some of the top IJNAF fighter pilots, including famous ace Sakai Saburo. The unit's Zeros deployed almost immediately from Lakunai to Lae, where some of its pilots are shown posing in late April. (Claringbould)

which included several top IJNAF pilots, arrived during April to take possession of the new fighters. The first nine deployed to Lae on April 14 and the others followed later in the month. The 25th Air Flotilla also included the 4th Air Group, now solely a bomber unit with 38 Bettys and 37 crews from the 4th, 1st, and Kisarazu Air Groups, and 12 flying boats and 13 crews of the Yokohama Air Group.

On the Allied side, the USAAF began to make its presence felt more strongly, with three units beginning operations that month. The 3rd and 22nd Bomb Groups and the 8th Fighter Group had been working up at various Australian bases with four aircraft types new to the theater. At Charters Towers, the 3rd Bomb Group's 8th Bomb Squadron flew Douglas A-24 dive-bombers, while its 13th Bomb Squadron was equipped with North American B-25Cs transferred from the Dutch. A Martin B-26 unit, the 22nd Bomb Group, became operational from Garbutt, while the 8th Fighter Group with P-39D/Fs trained up at Lowood near Brisbane to relieve No 75 Squadron at Seven Mile 'Drome. All of these units, along with the 19th Bomb Group, deployed aircraft to Port Moresby on April 5.

The RAAF struck the first major blow in April when No 75 Squadron strafed Lae on the 4th. A morning reconnaissance flight by the squadron commander revealed many aircraft parked along the runway, and he managed to damage three bombers in one pass. The squadron mounted a return strike that afternoon, during which, like in the morning attack, they managed to avoid the standing two-fighter patrol the Tainan Air Group flew over Lae in daytime. Five Kittyhawks approached at low altitude from over the Huon Gulf and destroyed two Zeros and damaged eight more, along with two bombers destroyed and at least seven damaged in one pass. This attack dented plans by the 25th Air Flotilla to launch

ORDER OF BATTLE, APRIL 1942

8TH FIGHTER GROUP		**22ND BOMB GROUP, B-26**	Garbutt
35th and 36th Fighter Sqns, P-39D	Port Moresby	No 75 Sqn, Kittyhawk	Port Moresby
3RD BOMB GROUP		No 11 and 20 Sqns, Catalina	Port Moresby
8th Bomb Sqn, A-24	Port Moresby	No 24 Sqn, Wirraway	Garbutt/Cairns
19TH BOMB GROUP, B-17E	Cloncurry/Garbutt	No 32 Sqn, Hudson	Port Moresby/Horn Island

a maximum-effort raid on Port Moresby the next day to soften up its defenses ahead of a seaborne assault planned for May.

The IJNAF attack went ahead on April 5, with seven Vunakanau Bettys escorted by four Lae Zeros scattering bombs around Seven Mile 'Drome from 15,000ft, but causing little damage. Coast watchers had sent a warning ahead of the attack and seven No 75 Squadron Kittyhawks rose to meet the raid, bypassing two escorts to attack the bombers from below just before they released their bombs. Though the 4th Air Group lost no bombers, a Tainan Air Group Zero was shot down; unusually, the pilot bailed out, but is believed to have later perished in the jungle. No Kittyhawks were damaged. The Japanese missed an opportunity by striking Seven Mile 'Drome too early; later, on April 5, USAAF aircraft arrived from Australia, along with seven replacement Kittyhawks for the 75th. Three B-17Es, five B-25Cs, eight B-26s, and five P-39Ds crowded the airfield, greatly straining its facilities – many crews slept in or under their planes. The same day, six A-24s flew into Three Mile 'Drome (Kila), joining six others that had deployed there on March 31.

The next day, the Allies mounted a major effort against Rabaul and Gasmata. It featured the first combat employment in the war of the B-25 and B-26. They, along with B-17Es, took off in darkness to hit their targets at dawn. Three B-17Es and eight B-26s made for Rabaul, while the five B-25Cs flew to Gasmata. The B-25Cs had a relatively easy inaugural mission, dropping 12,000lb of bombs and returning with one plane damaged by probable antiaircraft fire. Thick clouds over the Owen Stanleys forced two B-17Es and two B-26s to abort, despite the presence of experienced RAAF copilots in at least a few of the planes. The remainder reached the target area, but the results were meager. The lone B-17E bombed Vunakanau's runway, while the B-26s endured fruitless intercepts by relatively slow Claudes to attack shipping in Simpson Harbor at low altitude. None of the bombs found a ship. One B-26 was hit by antiaircraft fire from a ship and later ditched north of Kiriwina Island in the Louisiades; one crewman died in the ditching, but the others were picked up by a patrolling No 11 Squadron Catalina, the first of many such rescues during the campaign.

The 8th Fighter Group, which deployed a few pilots to Seven Mile 'Drome to gain experience flying alongside No 75 Squadron, also saw its first action. The 25th Air Flotilla sent seven Vunakanau Bettys and five Lae Zeros to Port Moresby in the morning, which they bombed from 20,000ft. Probably due to heavy clouds, their 84 bombs were widely scattered and did no damage. All the USAAF bombers that returned from the morning

Two 3rd Bomb Group squadrons, the 13th and 90th, began operations with conventionally configured B-25Cs. Here, a 90th Bomb Squadron aircraft operates at Seven Mile 'Drome in April 1942. As with B-26s, B-25Cs normally carried reduced bomb loads to ensure adequate fuel to survive New Guinea's high mountains and bad weather. (Claringbould)

missions to New Britain had already refueled and departed for their Australian bases, except for one B-17E damaged while taxiing, so the airfield was hardly a ripe target. Two of the 8th's five P-39Ds, along with seven No 75 Squadron Kittyhawks, scrambled to battle the attackers, but the Allies only damaged four Bettys, killing one crewman. Three Kittyhawks were damaged; two landed, but one ditched off Port Moresby. The pilot survived and the fighter was cannibalized for spare parts.

As USAAF fighter pilots entered the campaign, they flew generally in four-aircraft, two-element flights, with a flight leader and element leader each followed by a wingman to provide mutual protection. On both intercept and escort missions, they preferred to attack the Japanese from above, getting off quick bursts of fire, then diving to gain speed before zooming up to try for another pass. Maintenance of at least 250 knots airspeed was considered crucial to success in a fight.

The 3rd Bomb Group's A-24s, which were forced to abort an April 1 mission to Lae due to cloud cover, flew their first operation on April 7. Eight of the light bombers took off from Three Mile 'Drome in the morning, bound for Lae, with an escort of six No 75 Squadron Kittyhawks. Thick clouds at various altitudes initially kept Lae's patrolling Zeros from spotting the A-24s, but also caused the Kittyhawks to lose sight of their charges and return to Seven Mile 'Drome. The A-24s sighted at least seven Zeros and five bombers at the airfield and dove on them from 13,000ft, releasing their eight 500lb high explosive and 16 25lb incendiaries to good effect, with nine bombers claimed damaged. During the A-24s' egress, two patrolling Zeros pursued them, and each side lost an aircraft to enemy fire.

In mid-April, the B-25Cs and some B-17Es were diverted to support the Allied effort in the Philippines. On April 9, eight B-26s staged from Seven Mile 'Drome and attacked Simpson Harbor and Vunakanau airfield, using new tactics that presaged later Allied operations. Four bombed a transport from 4,500ft with 500lb bombs but missed. The other four bombed Vunakanau from only 500ft with 100lb fragmentation bombs, but all four were damaged by shrapnel from the explosions. One Betty was destroyed and eight damaged, added to 30 casualties among ground personnel. The B-26s flew five more missions, totaling 29 more sorties, during the rest of April against Rabaul-area targets, losing one aircraft to Zeros. In return, the transport *Komaki Maru* was sunk in Simpson Harbor on April 18, the first Japanese ship sunk by Allied land-based bombers in the SWPA. The ship's cargo of spare aircraft parts, fuel, and ammunition exploded, killing at least 80 crew and 11 Tainan Air Group ground personnel, also causing secondary explosions and fires in warehouses ashore. On April 30, three B-26s struck Lae, delivering 100lb bombs from about 600ft directly on the runway, destroying two Zeros. A-24s from the 3rd Bomb Group struck Lae on April 11 and 13, losing one on the former mission for serious damage to the merchantman *Taijun Maru* and destruction of a fuel dump. An escorting Kittyhawk and defending Zero were also lost on April 11; the Japanese pilot was killed, the Australian was captured and later executed. On the 13th, the dive-bombers returned to finish off *Taijun Maru*, but the ship had departed and the seven A-24s only inflicted minor damage at the airfield. Tainan Air Group patrols shot down one escorting Kittyhawk (the pilot was captured and later executed) and damaged another in exchange for minor damage to one Zero. Thereafter, A-24 missions were restricted by the reduction of No 75 Squadron's ability to provide enough aircraft for escort.

The Japanese scored a counterblow when patrolling Zeros shot down No 75 Squadron's commander, John Jackson, on a reconnaissance of Lae early on the morning of April 10, although he evaded capture and returned to the squadron two weeks later. Later that morning, seven Bettys and six Zeros only managed to destroy a truck at Seven Mile 'Drome with 70 bombs. However, they caused damage to the defending Kittyhawks, nine of which scrambled upon receiving a coast watcher's report of the incoming raid. Three remained on patrol against Zero strafers, while six engaged the raiders. Of these, Zeros damaged three, but one Betty was lost and another damaged.

The 3rd Bomb Group's 8th Bomb Squadron flew A-24 dive-bombers, with the unit's first mission coming on April 7. Because it was highly vulnerable to enemy fighters, it was only used sporadically, until a disastrous July 29 mission costing five of six aircraft led to its removal from combat operations. (Claringbould)

The 25th Air Flotilla paused raids on Port Moresby and returned all Bettys to the relative safety of Vunakanau on April 11. It had suffered heavy attrition and needed to replace losses from combat and Allied raids on Lae in early April in order to support the planned invasion of Port Moresby by sea in May. The 11th Air Fleet bolstered the 25th with the dispatch of the Tainan Air Group; the 11th Air Fleet also created the 5th Air Attack Force under the 25th Air Flotilla on April 10. The flotilla's authorized strength was an impressive 45 fighters, 63 bombers, 12 flying boats, and nine floatplanes. However, its actual strength during April fluctuated significantly due to losses and maintenance requirements, and was never more than 31 fighters (Zeros and Claudes), 25 bombers (Bettys and Nells), and 14 flying boats (Mavises). This made it very difficult for the 25th Air Flotilla to conduct the extensive reconnaissance demanded in preparation for Operation *MO* and still generate enough bombing sorties to suppress Allied air capabilities.

Despite its limitations, the 25th Air Flotilla renewed its offensive against Port Moresby on April 17, when 13 Zeros escorted five Bettys to attack a dispersal area at Seven Mile 'Drome with 132lb anti-personnel bombs. Only a couple of trucks and some fuel drums were destroyed. In the concurrent air battle, the Zeros destroyed one of two Kittyhawks en route to a morning reconnaissance of Lae and damaged three more Kittyhawks over Seven Mile 'Drome. One damaged Zero was written off upon crash-landing back at Lae, while No 75 Squadron lost a Kittyhawk that crashed upon takeoff. Both crashed pilots survived, but the pilot of the reconnaissance Kittyhawk was killed. The next day, 12 Lae Zeros on a sweep to Port Moresby met eight Kittyhawks that had scrambled to challenge them about 40 miles north of Seven Mile 'Drome. The Zeros used their altitude advantage to shoot down one enemy aircraft, killing the pilot, and damage another for no damage to themselves.

The 25th Air Flotilla struck Port Moresby again on April 23, first with a bombing of Seven Mile 'Drome by eight Bettys from 21,600ft that caused only minor damage, then later with a strafing run by three Zeros against the newly operational 12 Mile 'Drome (Bomana/Berry) and 14 Mile 'Drome (Laloki/Schwimmer). An afternoon sweep by two Zeros directed at 30 Mile 'Drome (Rorona/Rogers), then under construction, was aborted when six Kittyhawks rose to intercept. The next day saw the most successful operation for the Tainan Air Group in the entire campaign, when 12 Zeros conducted a morning sweep against Seven Mile 'Drome. Five strafed while seven provided cover. Two B-26s and a B-17E were

A 22nd Bomb Group B-26 sits at Seven Mile 'Drome during a 4th Air Group attack, probably on April 28, while a fuel dump burns. Early on during such attacks, USAAF aircraft often took off to avoid damage, but later practice was simply to wait out attacks on the ground. (Claringbould)

destroyed on the ground. A Catalina moored in the harbor was also destroyed by strafing. Two patrolling Kittyhawks dove at the Zeros, but the Zeros claimed one in a brief dogfight, with the pilot being saved. Four other Kittyhawks that had scrambled to meet the raid dove from 25,000ft once they sighted the strafers through the overcast. The Zeros broke upward to meet their attack and shot down another two Kittyhawks. One pilot was killed, while the other walked away from a forced landing that wrecked his plane. Allied non-combat losses this day were also serious. One B-17E aborted its mission and flew into a mountain, killing the crew. Three 3rd Bomb Group B-25Cs were lost at dusk after running out of fuel trying to stage from Cairns to Seven Mile 'Drome in rain squalls. All three ditched off the coast east of Port Moresby. Two crews were later rescued, but one B-25C that could not release its bombs exploded upon impact, killing the crew.

Keeping up the pressure, 15 Zeros again flew a sweep against Seven Mile and Three Mile 'Dromes on April 25. The Zeros endured intense antiaircraft fire at both locations, as well as an interception by four Kittyhawks. Two Kittyhawks and four Zeros were damaged, along with one B-26 on the ground. The following day saw another Tainan Air Group morning sweep over Seven Mile 'Drome, Port Moresby town, and the harbor. Seven Zeros again faced strong antiaircraft fire and four patrolling Kittyhawks. Four Zeros received minor damage, and two Kittyhawks were forced to land away from Seven Mile 'Drome low on fuel. About an hour later, nine Bettys and four Zeros bombed Three Mile 'Drome from 22,000ft and destroyed three A-24s. The Bettys also dropped a few bombs on the nearly completed 30 Mile 'Drome but caused no damage. On April 28, eight Bettys and 11 Zeros from Vunakanau were spotted by a coast watcher heading for Port Moresby. The bombers struck Seven Mile 'Drome, hitting a fuel dump and destroying an unserviceable Kittyhawk and a tractor. Five Kittyhawks climbed to attack the departing bombers and met Zeros diving to defend the bombers. One Zero was damaged and later ditched near Salamaua, with the pilot being rescued. The Zeros downed two Kittyhawks in a dogfight, one flown by the No 75 Squadron commander, John Jackson; both pilots were killed. Seven Mile 'Drome was later renamed "Jackson" in honor of the squadron commander. Later that day, a Zero was lost when it crash-landed after pursuing a reconnaissance B-25C leaving Lae, with the disoriented pilot being captured. Five 19th Bomb Group B-17Es followed up the B-25C sortie and bombed Lae through clouds, but caused only minor damage.

Bombs are delivered to arm a 22nd Bomb Group B-26 at Seven Mile 'Drome. B-26s deployed there from Garbutt for the type's first wartime operational mission on April 6. Thereafter, the B-26 served admirably, flying missions to Rabaul during April and May, as well as over New Guinea throughout the campaign. (NARA)

April closed with significant moves by both sides. April 29 was the emperor's 41st birthday, which the 25th Air Flotilla "celebrated" by sending nine Vunakanau Bettys and two sweeps of Lae Zeros to Port Moresby. The bombers did no damage dropping their small 132lb bombs through thick clouds just after noon. The sweeps, coming before and after the bombing attack, did a little better. Eight Zeros of the first sweep damaged a Hudson at Seven Mile 'Drome in exchange for three Zeros damaged by antiaircraft fire; six Zeros of the second sweep damaged two Kittyhawks and an A-24. This IJNAF effort was mounted despite a four-B-17E raid on Lae at 0700hrs, bombing from 20,000ft, that destroyed five Zeros and damaged four others for no loss, despite determined attacks by two patrolling Zeros. The next morning, of the nine B-26s that staged the previous night from Garbutt, mechanical problems meant only three could take off from Seven Mile 'Drome; these three bombed Lae from about 600ft and destroyed two Zeros before evading the Zeros launched to attack them. The 25th Air Flotilla responded the same morning by sending nine Vunakanau Bettys escorted by six Lae Zeros, all that were flyable, to hit Horn Island. The bombing with 90 132lb bombs was accurate but only destroyed two No 24 Squadron Wirraways. The escorting Zeros briefly chased and damaged a B-26 that got airborne just ahead of the raid. By April 30, relief for the depleted No 75 Squadron arrived at Seven Mile 'Drome in the form of 26 P-39D/Fs of the 8th Fighter Group's 35th and 36th Fighter Squadrons. Eleven of the newly arrived P-39s mounted a strafing attack on Lae and Salamaua during the afternoon of April 30. At Lae they destroyed three Zeros and damaged seven more, along with damaging ten Bettys and three small float planes moored in Huon Gulf. The American fighters also shot up supply dumps at Salamaua. After this success, a running fight proceeded all the way back to Seven Mile 'Drome with eight defending Zeros. One Zero was downed, with the pilot killed; one P-39 was destroyed (the pilot probably being captured and later executed) and three were forced to crash-land, with all the pilots being rescued.

Signals intelligence tipped off the Allies in mid-April that a major Japanese effort was pending (this was Operation *MO*). Intense Allied reconnaissance activity on May 1 and 3 – including Hudsons, Catalinas, and B-25Cs – confirmed a buildup of shipping at Rabaul. B-26s staged to Seven Mile 'Drome bombed Gasmata and Vunakanau on May 1 and 2, respectively, with limited results, for the loss of one B-26 that crash-landed in the Trobriand Islands, with two crew killed and the rest saved. One B-17E also tried to attack Rabaul on May 2, but was driven off by a Zero. Two B-17Es tried again on May 3, when their

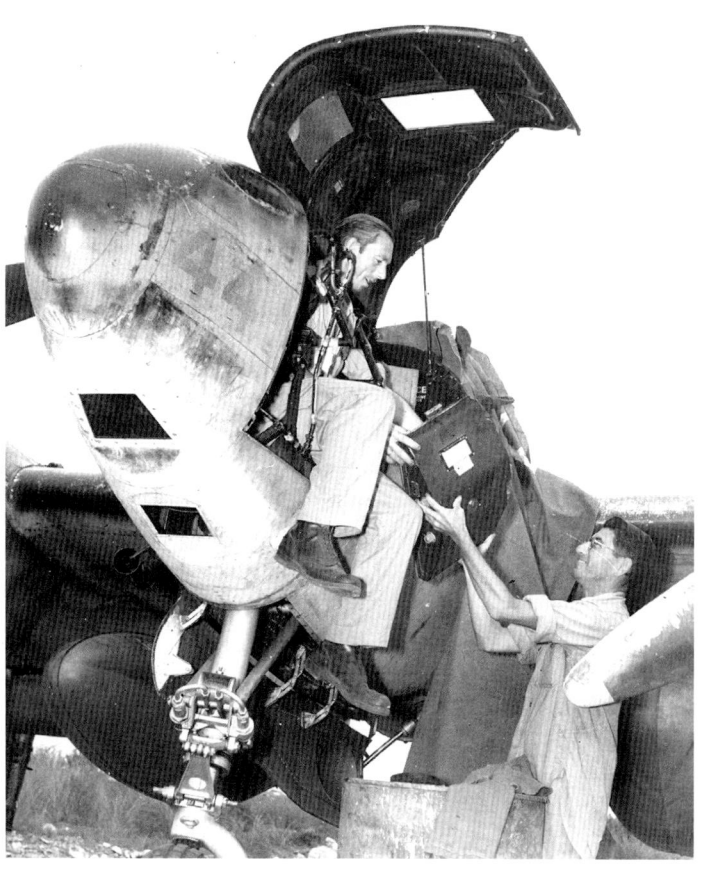

An 8th Photo Reconnaissance Squadron F-4A has film removed from its nose cameras. The unit's tactical intelligence was critical to the Allied effort. After an initial operational loss in May, the unit gained experience and moved from Australia to 14 Mile 'Drome on September 9 to support operations more effectively. (Claringbould)

eight 500lb bombs all missed the 20-plus ships sighted in Simpson Harbor. That same day, a Yokohama Air Group Mavis on reconnaissance traded gunfire with a 3rd Bomb Group B-25C also reconnoitering east of New Guinea, with both being damaged. Of note, a new USAAF reconnaissance unit made its operational debut on May 4 when an 8th Photo Reconnaissance Squadron F-4A departed Townsville, refueled at 14 Mile 'Drome, and headed for Lae and Rabaul. The F-4A was lost with its pilot to unknown causes – possibly bad weather; this loss, coupled with a crash-landing of another F-4A in Australia, led to the withdrawal of the unit from operations until late July.

The Japanese reinforced units at Rabaul ahead of Operation *MO*. Nine Genzan Air Group Nells arrived from Truk on April 20. On May 1, the 25th Air Flotilla's 5th Air Attack Force had a serviceable strength of 18 Zeros, six Claudes, 17 Bettys, 25 Nells, and 12 Mavises. Zeros flew strafing runs against Seven Mile 'Drome on May 1 and 2; on the latter mission they shot down a No 75 Squadron fighter and the pilot was killed. No 75 Squadron flew its last mission on May 3, when its remaining flyable Kittyhawk joined eight 8th Fighter Group P-39s to meet 14 Bettys and nine Zeros over Seven Mile 'Drome. The Kittyhawk aborted due to engine overheating, but the dogfight claimed a P-39D and its pilot in exchange for two Bettys damaged (one crash-landed at Lae); their bombing resulted in minimal damage. The P-39s flew a strike against Lae on the morning of May 4. Ten fighters took off, but bad weather over the mountains forced five to abort. After damaging four Bettys, the other five P-39s ran into defending Zeros. One P-39 was shot down and another three were probably victims of the weather, with all the pilots being killed. That day also saw the last IJNAF raid on Port Moresby for a week, as nine Bettys again bombed Seven Mile 'Drome without result, while eight P-39s fought nine Zeros for the loss of one pilot killed in the dogfight and another injured in a crash upon takeoff. As of May 4, No 75 Squadron ceased operations and the 8th Fighter Group had lost 12 aircraft, with seven pilots killed and one seriously injured, in less than a week of operations, leading the Japanese to believe that they had effectively suppressed Allied fighters at Port Moresby.

The battle of attrition continues

The battle of the Coral Sea from May 5–8 engaged the majority of the 25th Air Flotilla's attention. But the 25th's operations over New Guinea persisted, with 21 IJNAF raids during May, most of them fighter sweeps/strafing runs. This included a May 11 raid on Horn Island by nine Bettys and nine Zeros that only destroyed a No 24 Squadron Wirraway and a few buildings. That same day, a major attack by 19 Genzan Air Group Nells and eight Lae Zeros on Seven Mile 'Drome caused little damage. Another big effort was mounted on May 18 against Port Moresby, featuring 18 Nells and 16 Bettys escorted by seven Zeros from

Lakunai and 11 from Lae. The Bettys' bombs were dropped wide of Seven Mile 'Drome, but the Nells squarely hit 12 Mile 'Drome and destroyed two P-39s, damaged another, and cratered the runway. P-39s had scrambled ahead of the raid and the ensuing air battle resulted in two Bettys being destroyed, one in a collision with a P-39F (the aircraft later crashed with its pilot) and the other which crash-landed at Lae; six Bettys received minor damage. Yokohama Air Group Mavises made two- or three-plane nighttime raids on May 25, 26, and 27, but only minor damage to Seven Mile 'Drome resulted. The Tainan Air Group was more effective during the month, destroying one B-25, one A-24, and two P-40Es on the ground and also destroying nine P-39s and damaging six P-39s and one B-26 in air combat, at a cost of seven Zeros lost and at least three damaged. On May 13, the experienced Tainan pilots first used the tactic of head-on passes at B-17Es to take advantage of their weak nose defenses. During May, the 25th Air Flotilla received 43 new Zeros. This allowed at least two dozen to be routinely stationed at Lae, and several of the sweeps in the last half of the month comprised as many as 15–26 fighters. For its part, the 8th Fighter Group received enough replacements in May to have 20 P-39s and 26 pilots on strength at the end of the month.

Allied counterattacks in May targeted the Rabaul area six times, while Lae and Salamaua received a combined nine bomber attacks. Attacks against shipping in Simpson Bay and Huon Gulf were ineffective. Airfield strikes were somewhat more effective, but at a steep cost. Between May 13 and 28, three Zeros were destroyed – two from defensive fire and one on the ground – while one Betty and three Nells were damaged for the loss of ten B-25Cs and two B-26s, with 40 crewmen being killed. Bad weather was a major factor in these meager results, despite low-altitude bombing being used on multiple occasions. After May 24, no more B-26s were sent on Rabaul missions due to a combination of the extreme range and their relatively small bomb loads.

One bright spot for the Allies came on May 26 when, foreshadowing many future Allied operations, USAAF 21st Troop Carrier Squadron transport aircraft, staged from Archerfield near Brisbane, flew the Australian 2/5th Independent Company from Port Moresby into Wau

Various Nell units augmented the 11th Air Fleet's Bettys during the campaign in attacking Port Moresby. This is a formation of Genzan Air Group Nells returning from Port Moresby, probably in May. They carried a 1,764lb external bomb load, and though obsolescent suffered only five combat losses during the campaign. (Claringbould)

Two 8th Fighter Group P-39Ds scramble from Seven Mile 'Drome, probably in May, while B-26s sit in the background. Despite coast-watcher reports and crude radar detection, Allied fighters often lacked sufficient warning time of 11th Air Fleet raids to intercept the bombers before they reached their Port Moresby targets. (Claringbould)

to bolster its small garrison. Five transports, escorted by P-39s, took advantage of good weather to make several runs in support of what became known as Kanga Force. Sixteen Tainan Air Group Zeros attempted to oppose the operation, but instead tangled with seven 8th Fighter Group P-39s which, for the loss of one plane and pilot, held off the Japanese so the operation could succeed.

June saw fewer attacks by each side but also some new tactics. The 8th Fighter Group flew its last mission on June 1, suffering the last three of 26 fighters and the final two of 13 pilots lost during its stint at Port Moresby. Forewarned, 30 P-39s were launched with enough time to gain an altitude advantage on the approaching Japanese. They dove on 18 Nells and 21 Zeros that attacked Port Moresby's wharf around noon, destroying one Zero. The Japanese bombing damaged one ship and many buildings. The next day, the two 8th Fighter Group squadrons at Port Moresby were relieved by the 35th Fighter Group's 39th and 40th Fighter Squadrons, flying mainly P-400s. Following the 8th Fighter Group's practice with No 75 Squadron in April, some 35th Fighter Group pilots flew familiarization sorties alongside the 8th earlier in May. The 35th dispersed its fighters to free space for bombers at Seven Mile 'Drome, with the 39th Fighter Squadron at 12 Mile and 14 Mile 'Dromes and the 40th Fighter Squadron at Five Mile 'Drome (Ward's).

On June 9, Allied bombers targeted Lae with a one-two punch. Two B-17Es and five B-25Cs from Seven Mile 'Drome arrived over Lae in the morning and bombed the wharf through thick but broken cloud. The B-25Cs stayed at 16,000ft in a tactical change from their previous costly low-level efforts. Twenty-four Zeros attacked the B-25Cs as they fled eastward, and then ran into ten B-26s heading for a second strike on Lae, one of which was carrying then-Congressman and later President Lyndon Johnson (his aircraft aborted due to a mechanical problem before reaching the target). The B-26s dropped their bombs on Salamaua instead and turned for home at low level over the Huon Gulf. One B-26 was shot down with the crew lost, but all B-17Es and B-25Cs returned. Two Zeros and their pilots were lost when they ran into P-400s executing the new tactic of orbiting at various altitudes over Cape Ward Hunt to catch Zeros chasing returning Allied bombers. One P-400 crash-landed on the southeast coast, with the pilot later returning to the 35th Fighter Group.

During this mission, the bombers spotted a Tainan Air Group Babs at Lae. The high-speed asset was slated to conduct reconnaissance to improve the 25th Air Flotilla's rather spotty intelligence of Allied air strength in New Guinea and Australia. Another new IJNAF type was the Nakajima A6M2-N "Rufe" seaplane fighter flown by the Yokohama Air Group's fighter element. Twelve Rufes arrived at Rabaul on June 3, and for about a month flew harbor defensive patrols before moving to Tulagi. Six of these attacked five B-17Es on a fruitless June 10 Rabaul mission, but no losses occurred on either side.

Major combat took place on June 16. In the morning, 21 Lae Zeros on a sweep used an altitude advantage to bounce 32 P-400s directly over Seven Mile 'Drome. For no losses to themselves, the Zeros shot down five P-400s, killing two of the pilots, and seriously damaged two more, the largest single-day P-39/P-400 loss in the entire campaign. Meanwhile, four B-17Es and 12 B-25Cs left Seven Mile 'Drome ahead of the Zero sweep to bomb Lae and Salamaua, respectively. Twelve B-26s took off as the Zeros appeared and orbited over water until the raid ended. They then flew to bomb Lae and tried to catch the refueling Zeros on the ground. The bombing by both groups cratered the runways at the two airfields and likely damaged several aircraft at Lae. In the subsequent defensive pursuit of the B-26s, one Zero was shot down by the waiting P-400s over Cape Ward Hunt. No bombers or P-400s were lost.

Large 25th Air Flotilla raids against Port Moresby between June 17 and 19 targeted shipping in the harbor instead of the airfields. These succeeded in destroying the 4,561-ton cargo ship *Macdhui* that had just delivered aviation fuel. During the fighter skirmish on the 18th, Lae Zeros shot down three P-400s, with all the pilots bailing out. Two night raids by Mavises were flown on June 24 and 25, the first targeting Seven Mile 'Drome resulting in no damage and the second being aborted en route due to weather. A 21-Zero sweep at noon on June 25 netted only one P-39F, written off in a crash-landing at 12 Mile 'Drome. Another daylight raid on June 26 likewise resulted in no damage to Seven Mile 'Drome, despite 20 Nells delivering their bombs. In two separate fights, 11 escorting Zeros downed one P-39 near the target, killing the pilot, while a little later the P-39s/P-400s caught up with the departing Nells near Kokoda and damaged eight, one of which was written off upon crash-landing at Lae.

Allied counter-raids later in June, several at night, produced inconclusive results. Attackers noted fires at Rabaul after night attacks by three No 11 Squadron Catalinas on June 20 and seven 19th Bomb Group B-17Es on June 24. Seven No 100 Squadron Beauforts, deployed to Port Moresby, flew their first bombing mission of the campaign on the night of June 25–26

A No 100 Squadron Beaufort at Five Mile 'Drome in late June 1942. The unit began operations that month but was soon withdrawn to Australia for additional training, returning to Milne Bay in September. Its maritime strike operations were unsuccessful, attributed in part to malfunctions experienced with the US Navy's Mk XIII torpedoes. (Claringbould)

A 39th Fighter Squadron P-400 damaged during the 4th Air Group's July 5 attack on Seven Mile 'Drome. The P-39s and P-400s performed most of the Allied fighter defense of Port Moresby throughout 1942, and while creditable ground-attack aircraft they were decidedly inferior to the Zero in a dogfight. (NARA)

in conjunction with 3rd Bomb Group B-25Cs against Salamaua and Lae. Salamaua was strafed by the B-25Cs, while five Beauforts bombed ships and antiaircraft sites near Lae. Little damage was done, and no ships were hit. One Beaufort became lost on the return flight and crashed into a mountain, while another was damaged by ships' antiaircraft fire. Five 22nd Bomb Group B-26s bombed Lae and Salamaua on the night of June 27–28 in terrible weather, with no reported results, returning to Seven Mile 'Drome with one damaged by antiaircraft fire. This was the only night B-26 mission of the campaign.

An Australian commando raid on a former missionary site near Lae early on July 1 sparked Japanese reprisal bombing and strafing attacks on and near Bulolo and Wau on July 2 and 3. Allied pressure on Lae and Salamaua continued with B-17E, B-25C, and B-26 raids on July 1, 3, 4, and 5, causing little damage due to adverse weather. The major July 4 operation, with many aircraft staged to Seven Mile 'Drome, consisted of four Catalinas, four Hudsons, six B-17Es, seven B-25Cs, and 16 B-26s. An earlier night "nuisance" attack by two Bettys on Seven Mile 'Drome caused no damage. A Tainan Air Group sweep with 20 Zeros later that morning met 13 39th Fighter Squadron P-400s, and a dogfight north of Port Moresby resulted in the loss of three P-400s and two damaged, with all pilots saved – no Zeros were lost. The Allied bombings that day of Lae and Salamaua occurred in relays, with large fires reported at Lae. One Zero and one B-26 were lost in a midair collision, killing all aircrew, and a Hudson failed to return due to unknown causes, but otherwise there were no combat losses. Raids by each side over the next two weeks destroyed two B-26s, a P-39, a Hudson on the ground, an ammunition dump, two P-400s shot down with the pilots killed, and a Zero and Betty shot down with all aircrew killed.

Tactical reconnaissance intensified on both sides. The Tainan Air Group received three Nakajima J1N1-C "Irvings" by July 20. The group's Babs were also very active from mid-June, expanding the 25th Air Flotilla's understanding of Allied dispositions in northern Australia. They also gathered information on viable overland routes from the northern shore of Papua to Port Moresby.

For the Allies, the 19th Bomb Group's 435th Bomb Squadron (redesignated from 40th Bomb Squadron on April 9), tasked mainly with armed reconnaissance, had begun deploying four crews and two planes full time to Seven Mile 'Drome in June. The squadron received three extended-range LB-30s in June and July to take some of the load off its ageing B-17Es. The 435th also received radar and night photography equipment for its B-17Es. Allied reconnaissance missions were often flown as "cover" for intelligence received by other means. These additions were timely, since intelligence gleaned from the July 1 Lae commando raid and US Navy communication intercepts indicated that the Japanese were planning a major operation, probably on New Guinea, in the latter half of July.

The Japanese invasion of Buna

MacArthur had foreseen in May that the Allies would need to build up forces in northern and eastern Papua to halt expected Japanese operations to take Port Moresby. While the battle of the Coral Sea had, in MacArthur's view, defused any immediate danger of a Japanese invasion of Australia, it also sharpened Allied perceptions of the danger in delaying development of additional facilities on New Guinea for defending the island. Likewise, the Coral Sea setback fueled the IGHQ's determination to pursue an overland assault against Port Moresby (Operation *RE*) that required a buildup of forces. Thus began a race between the combatants to occupy suitable territory to build additional airfields and other infrastructure from which to mount decisive attacks against the enemy. A prime goal for each side was to establish an air presence at Buna on the northeast coast.

Despite MacArthur's pressure on Allied ground commanders to occupy Buna, the Japanese got there first. Late on July 21, the 17th Army's Yokoyama Advance Force of about 1,800 IJA and IJN troops, plus 1,300 IJN and native laborers, landed from three transports at Buna and Gona under cover of severe weather. The invasion convoy withstood Allied air attacks that scored no hits. There was no morning IJNAF fighter cover of the invasion force on July 22 due to the weather, allowing determined Allied aerial opposition that day. A 435th Bomb Squadron B-17E flew under the 1,000ft ceiling and disabled the transport *Ayotosan Maru* in the morning, then loitered for three hours providing position and weather information to other Allied aircraft. A Hudson, ten B-17Es, six B-25Cs, and five B-26s all made morning attacks on the landing force but caused little discernible damage.

Over the rest of July, as the Yokoyama Advance Force pushed southwest and captured Kokoda, bad weather severely limited the Allies' ability to effectively strike either the ground force or its maritime resupply convoys. From July 23–31, the Allies flew a total of five Hudson, three Catalina, seven Kittyhawk, 26 A-24, 16 B-17E, 21 B-25C, 31 B-26, and six P-39/400 sorties against the invasion force and shipping, managing only to damage the destroyer *Asanagi* on July 26 and, after two attempts, to disable ammunition on the carrier *Kotoku Maru* on July 30, though its cargo was mostly salvaged. Weather, Tainan Air Group Zeros from Lae, and antiaircraft fire downed or caused to be written off four P-39s/P-400s, one Hudson, two B-25Cs, and five A-24s, with 25 aircrew killed. The bad weather showed no favoritism, also hampering attacks by 4th Air Group Bettys, which targeted Port Moresby's airfields four times during the same period but only managed to destroy one Hudson at Seven Mile 'Drome and ammunition and fuel dumps at 12 Mile 'Drome, suffering no bomber or fighter losses in return.

However, the Allied air threat did force the Japanese to move troops only at night. A visiting IGHQ IJA staff officer who was wounded on the *Asanagi* reported on July 28 to the 25th Air Flotilla and the IGHQ's Army Department his view that the Allies had gained air superiority over Buna. In response to the growing Allied air operations, the 8th Fleet, which was established at Rabaul on July 27 to oversee all South Pacific operations, and the 17th Army agreed on July 31 that the IJNAF would base aircraft at Buna to better support

This 22nd Bomb Group B-26 crash-landed on July 22 at Seven Mile 'Drome, after receiving antiaircraft damage. It had been hit while attacking Japanese sea transports at Gona about 0900hrs, but without success because of clouds and rain over the target. (Claringbould)

the ground campaign. But since Buna was only 20 minutes flight time from Port Moresby, this proximity to the front became a double-edged sword, making IJNAF aircraft deployed there easier Allied targets.

Both sides fed reinforcements into the battle during July. The IJNAF's 14th Air Group based four H8K1 "Emily" flying boats at Rabaul to conduct long-range bombing and reconnaissance. They flew three bombing missions to Townsville on the nights of July 25–26, 27–28, and 28–29, two to Horn Island on July 29–30 and July 31 – August 1, and one to Cairns on July 30–31. These raids totaled eight Emily sorties that only resulted in damage to four No 32 Squadron Hudsons at Horn Island. The Allies moved two Kittyhawk squadrons – Nos 75 and 76 – to Milne Bay and two P-39/P-400 squadrons – the 8th Fighter Group's 80th Fighter Squadron and the 35th Fighter Group's 41st Fighter Squadron – went to Port Moresby to relieve the 35th Fighter Group's 39th and 40th Fighter Squadrons, which departed on July 30. All these American units, along with No 76's Kittyhawks staging from Seven Mile 'Drome, saw action on July 22 against the invasion force and Lae-based Zeros.

Early August saw just one major IJNAF raid on Port Moresby. On August 1, six Bettys bombed Seven Mile 'Drome at night, but due to poor weather and darkness they caused no damage for the loss of one Betty through unknown causes. Later that day, 19th Bomb Group B-17Es bombed a resupply convoy en route to Buna devoid of air cover due to weather. The attack damaged no ships but did cause the convoy to return to Rabaul. The weather improved sufficiently the following day to allow nine Lae Zeros to intercept and shoot down one of five 28th Bomb Squadron B-17Es flying under the clouds looking for the convoy, for the loss of one Zero. Five B-26s and three 41st Fighter Squadron P-400s heading for Buna encountered the same Zeros; two P-400s were shot down, with the pilots killed, and the B-26s were scattered before they could drop their bombs. The 41st did have one success that morning when it shot down a Tainan Air Group Irving heading to Port Moresby on a reconnaissance flight, the first combat loss of this type in the war.

A 41st Fighter Squadron P-400 is readied for a mission from Seven Mile 'Drome, with a No 76 Squadron Kittyhawk behind its fuselage. This photo was taken on July 22, prior to a mission that afternoon against the Japanese landing at Buna-Gona, during which eight P-400s escorted seven 500lb bomb-laden Kittyhawks. (NARA)

In the first week of August, the Allies flew several raids on Lae and Salamaua to keep the Japanese from noting the buildup of B-17Es at Port Moresby, ordered by Kenney to support the impending American invasion of Guadalcanal. Catalinas bombed at night on August 2, 3, and 6–7, and a total of 53 daylight sorties by B-26s, B-25Cs, and B-17Es on August 6, 7, and 8 repeatedly damaged the two airfields.

Allied pressure on Lae and Salamaua prompted the Japanese to temporarily recall the Zeros based there to Rabaul on August 3, then on August 6, the 25th Air Flotilla gained 15 Zeros (the shorter-range A6M3 variant) and 16 Vals of the 2nd Air Group. An additional 20 A6M3s were delivered by sea on July 29. Lastly, the 26th Air Flotilla sent its Misawa Air Group of 27 Bettys, optimistically earmarked for Guadalcanal basing, to Vunakanau by August 9.

Allied raids on Rabaul continued as the land battles on New Guinea and in the Solomons unfolded. In addition to a two-Catalina "nuisance" raid before dawn on August 9, four 19th Bomb Group B-17Es from Seven Mile 'Drome bombed Lakunai just before dark; a fifth with engine trouble turned back early and bombed Gasmata. One B-17E was shot down around 1800hrs by 14 defending Tainan Air Group Zeros, crashing on New Britain and killing the crew. Another succumbed later to battle damage and low fuel and ditched off Milne Bay, with the crew rescued by the Royal Australian Navy. Another raid on August 12 targeted the large number of ships in Simpson Harbor, some of which were intended to resupply the Yokoyama Advance Force. Seven B-17Es bombed from 26,000ft, inflicting minor damage to one transport, while 15 Zeros slightly damaged some of the attackers for no damage to themselves. The supply convoy left that same day but was spotted on August 13 by Allied reconnaissance. Coincidentally, 16 Zeros redeployed to Lae on the same day, and these provided air cover for the convoy approaching Buna. Due to clouds, they missed seven B-17Es which attacked the convoy that morning. As was almost always the case, the B-17s caused no damage and the convoy unloaded that night and departed for Rabaul. Nine Zeros intercepted B-26s attacking Buna that afternoon and, although the bombers were escorted by 8th Fighter Group P-400s, damaged two B-26s, with one being forced to ditch. The next day, one B-17E and one Zero were lost during fruitless attempts to attack the returning convoy.

This sequence captures the 22nd Bomb Group's attack on Lae airfield from 3,400ft on August 7. In the picture above, smoke rises from the runway and dispersal areas just after bombing, while in the lower picture a B-26 heads south after the attack. Though a few IJNAF aircraft are just visible to the right of the runway between smoke clouds in the upper picture, 11th Air Fleet had recalled most aircraft to Rabaul on August 3. (MacArthur Memorial)

Seven 19th Bomb Group B-17E/Fs attacked Rabaul's Simpson Harbor on August 12. Although Allied day and night bombing of Simpson Harbor rarely resulted in sinkings, they did damage both ships and port facilities. The Allies kept steady though generally small-scale pressure on the harbor to disrupt Japanese invasion and resupply efforts. (NARA)

On August 17, the 25th Air Flotilla made its first major raid from Rabaul on Port Moresby since August 1. Nine 4th Air Group and 16 Misawa Air Group Bettys, escorted by 12 Tainan Air Group and ten 2nd Air Group Zeros, bombed Seven Mile 'Drome after executing an unusual approach from the east. This route precluded fighter interception, and antiaircraft fire was only able to damage five Bettys. The accurate bombing destroyed one B-26, five transport aircraft, the control tower, and operations hut, also damaging one B-26 and four transports. Damage to the transport force was an especially severe blow to Australian ground troops' ability to resist the 17th Army's advance on Kokoda, as these troops were being supplied principally by air. To make up for the shortfall, No 32 Squadron Hudsons (which had flown their last bombing sortie of the campaign on July 30), a B-17D, and six A-24s were pressed into transport duties.

In addition to sustained USAAF attacks on Buna, the final week of August saw two raids on Rabaul. The first was a night mission against Vunakanau in very bad weather on August 24–25 by eight B-17Es. The second was a daylight August 29 strike on Vunakanau by seven B-17E/Fs. No combat losses resulted for either side from these raids. An August 31 attack on Lae saw the operational debut of the 3rd Bomb Group's 89th Bomb Squadron, forward-based at Three Mile 'Drome and equipped with modified Douglas A-20As. In the August 31 attack, nine B-26s bombed Lae first from 5,500ft, while 13 A-20As strafed and bombed the airfield with parafrags at low level immediately afterwards. Low-level attacks by aircraft modified for the purpose was a tactic the Allies would perfect in coming months.

Milne Bay – Japan's first defeat on the ground

Having lost the race to Buna, the Allies found it imperative to secure eastern Papua. In a May 20 directive, MacArthur had ordered the establishment of an airfield in the Abau–Mullins Harbor area of southeastern Papua, roughly midway between Port Moresby and Samarai Island, that could support heavy bomber operations. However, in June, US Army engineers found a better site at a coconut plantation near Gili Gili on Milne Bay. Construction of three airfields began on June 29, and by late July, the first, originally called No 1 strip but later christened Gurney strip, was able to accommodate fighters. The site had a garrison of two

These 89th Bomb Squadron A-20As leave Three Mile 'Drome on a mission in late 1942. The unit formed part of the 5th Air Force's "strike group" that relentlessly attacked targets in the Buna area, Lae and Salamaua airfields, and resupply convoys such as that attacked in the Bismarck Sea in March 1943. (Claringbould)

companies of Australian infantry, US Army engineers and antiaircraft artillerymen, Nos 75 and 76 Kittyhawk squadrons, and detachments of Hudsons from Nos 6 and 32 Squadrons. By mid-August, the garrison had grown to 8,824 men, including personnel of RAAF No 37 Radar Station, which set up radar providing limited coverage east of the airfield, and the USAAF 8th Fighter Control Squadron, making its first theater deployment in preparation for a future move of the 8th Fighter Group to Milne Bay. While the 8th Fighter Control Squadron used No 37's radar data to direct fighter interceptions, it also relied heavily on radio reports from coast watchers.

The Allies had won the race to secure eastern Papua. It was not until late July that the Japanese 8th Fleet decided to invade extreme eastern Papua. On August 3, a 4th Air Group Betty conducting reconnaissance for potential invasion points and a future seaplane base at Samarai Island stumbled upon the Milne Bay base. The next day, a reconnaissance Babs escorted by four Tainan Air Group Zeros returned to get better information. A brief clash ensued with eight patrolling Kittyhawks of No 76 Squadron, during which the Babs was shot down in exchange for two No 76 Squadron fighters damaged and one No 75 Squadron Kittyhawk destroyed on the ground by two strafing Zeros. Though detailed photos of the Milne Bay base were lost with the Babs, the two missions allowed the 25th Air Flotilla to determine the general layout of the airfield and docking facilities, and to estimate that approximately 39 Kittyhawks were based at the field.

In response to this unexpected development, the 25th Air Flotilla planned a maximum effort against Milne Bay for August 7. This attack force comprised 27 4th Air Group Bettys and 17 Tainan Air Group Zeros, virtually every aircraft of each type available. However, the force was diverted to deal with the American landing on Guadalcanal that same day. Meanwhile, in concert with the Guadalcanal landing, the 19th Bomb Group executed a maximum effort raid ordered by Kenney against Vunakanau because Allied intelligence had reported a total of 150 aircraft there and at other Rabaul-area airfields. Sixteen B-17E/Fs staged to Seven Mile 'Drome late on August 6, and despite a takeoff accident and two mechanical aborts the 19th still managed to put 13 B-17E/Fs over Vunakanau around noon on August 7. After running a defensive gauntlet of 11 Tainan Air Group and

15 2nd Air Group Zeros, the B-17s hit Vunakanau from 22,000ft with 96 500lb bombs. Since the morning Japanese raid against Guadalcanal had already departed, no aircraft were destroyed in the attack and the airfield itself suffered little damage. Twelve B-17E/Fs, some damaged, returned to base in Australia, one having been shot down by the newly arrived Zeros.

Japanese operations against Guadalcanal during August delayed their planned seaborne assault on Milne Bay and limited aircraft availability to conduct pre-invasion attacks against Milne Bay and Port Moresby. Japanese reconnaissance of Milne Bay was plagued by bad weather, leading the 8th Fleet to grossly underestimate the size of the Allied garrison. Thus, the plan to land only 1,533 IJN troops seemed acceptable.

On August 11, the only Japanese air attack launched to soften up Milne Bay prior to the planned invasion was limited by the weather and aircraft availability. This attack was planned for midday by 12 4th Air Group Bettys and 15 Tainan Air Group Zeros, preceded a half hour earlier by seven 2nd Air Group Zeros to clear away any patrolling Allied fighters ahead of the main attack. However, rain squalls and low clouds forced most of the attack force to return to Rabaul. Only six Zeros continued the mission to carry out strafing runs against the airfield. The Japanese were tracked by coast watchers and No 37 Radar Station approaching at low altitude from the east, and were met by 22 Kittyhawks of Nos 75 and 76 Squadrons. In the sharp combat that ensued in and out of low-lying clouds, the Zeros, after a strafing pass at the airfield, took advantage of their superior skill against the more numerous yet relatively inexperienced Australians. In the resulting dogfight, Zeros downed one No 75 Squadron and three No 76 Squadron Kittyhawks, with all of their pilots being killed. One damaged Zero ditched near Buna on its return flight and the pilot was rescued.

The Allies were ready for the Japanese invasion, having been alerted by communications intelligence to expect a major action between August 22 and 27. In preparation, the Japanese began using Buna airfield on August 18 and staged the 2nd Air Group's A6M3s there on August 22. The 25th Air Flotilla was also bolstered by the 26th Air Flotilla's Kisarazu Air Group Bettys based at Kavieng on New Ireland. On August 23, the 25th Air Flotilla sent eight Val dive-bombers and eight Zeros from Rabaul and eight Zeros from Buna to attack Milne Bay, but weather foiled the mission and only a brief encounter between the Buna Zeros and a patrolling No 75 Squadron Kittyhawk occurred, resulting in the loss of a Zero in a landing accident at Buna. The next day saw a similar outcome as 14 Bettys – seven each from the 4th and Kisarazu Air Groups – along with Zeros from both the Tainan and 2nd Air Groups, launched a morning raid on Milne Bay. Although the bombers were again thwarted by adverse weather and returned to Rabaul with their bombs still aboard, the Zeros managed to mix it up with 26 Kittyhawks from Nos 75 and 76 Squadrons. A single fighter from each side was damaged.

By August 24, the main Japanese invasion force embarking the Kure 3rd and most of the Sasebo 5th SNLFs was en route to Milne Bay from Rabaul. A secondary force of elements of the Sasebo 5th SNLF on barges departed Buna to execute a landing at Taupota on the northeastern Papuan coast, moving at night to avoid air attack. However, the barge force was spotted by coast watchers at Porlock Harbor on the 24th. The Japanese stopped at Goodenough Island on August 25, planning to proceed to Taupota that night, but could not

The 11th Air Fleet used bombers and flying boats for long-range reconnaissance but employed the "Babs", "Irving," and "Dinah" for tactical reconnaissance. This Tainan Air Group Babs usually operated from Rabaul, but occasionally deployed to Lae. A Babs was lost on August 4 while reconnoitering the Allied buildup at Milne Bay. (Claringbould)

A No 76 Squadron Kittyhawk taxis on a Marston mat at a soggy Gurney strip. Kittyhawks of Nos 75 and 76 Squadrons fought a tenacious battle in late August 1942 against the Milne Bay invasion force, stranding part of it en route at Goodenough Island and playing a critical role in defeating the Japanese who did land at the bay. (Claringbould)

adequately camouflage their barges. A coast watcher on Goodenough reported their presence that morning, and in the early afternoon nine No 75 Squadron Kittyhawks strafed the seven barges and destroyed them all, along with much equipment and the force's sole radio. The attack kept this portion of the Sasebo 5th SNLF out of the Milne Bay fight, and it remained stranded until being mopped up by Australian forces in late October. On August 25, the Allies attacked both Buna and the main invasion convoy, located that morning by a Kitava Island coast watcher as well as No 6 Squadron and 435th Bomb Squadron reconnaissance aircraft. Before dawn, 32 P-39s/P-400s – 16 each from the 8th and 35th Fighter Groups – set out for Buna, but due to heavy rain and a 100ft ceiling all but four returned to Port Moresby without locating the target. The remaining four 35th Fighter Group P-400s found Buna and made one strafing pass, leaving three Zeros burning. A follow-up attack by seven 35th Fighter Group P-400s later in the morning found improved weather, which allowed them to destroy two more aircraft. After these attacks, the 2nd Air Group was left with only six serviceable Zeros at Buna.

Attacks on the invasion convoy – consisting of two troop transports, two light cruisers, three destroyers, and two sub chasers – began during the afternoon, with six No 75 Squadron Kittyhawks led to the target by a No 6 Squadron Hudson. Though none of the pilots had any dive-bombing training, the Kittyhawks strafed and dropped 250lb bombs despite heavy rain and a 1,000ft cloud ceiling. The attack was predictably unsuccessful, as were two others, one by three Kittyhawks from No 75 and six from No 76 Squadrons, and the second by a No 6 Squadron Hudson that dropped four 250lb and three 100lb bombs from very low altitude. The Japanese lost 20 personnel killed but suffered virtually no damage to the convoy. One No 76 Squadron Kittyhawk ditched for lack of fuel, but the pilot was rescued. After reaching the target area, the Japanese landing began on the north shore of Milne Bay just after midnight on August 26. By dawn, the main Japanese invasion force was ashore near Waga Waga, almost 5 miles east of the Allied base.

During the critical day of the landing, the Japanese were unable to provide air support to their invasion force. Though the 25th Air Flotilla deployed a strike force from Rabaul to Buna in the morning to support the operation, the six Zeros and eight Vals were unable to support the ground troops later in the day owing to bad weather, landing back at Buna in the afternoon. Buna had been strafed earlier that morning by six 80th Fighter Squadron P-400s

An A6M3 Zero of the 2nd Air Group damaged at Buna on August 26. The unit deployed there to allow its shorter-range A6M3s to take advantage of the proximity of Buna to Port Moresby and Milne Bay, but by September 8, Allied attacks caused the IJNAF to abandon Buna permanently. (Claringbould)

that caught ten 2nd Air Group Zeros bound for Milne Bay during takeoff. The Americans shot down three, killing the pilots, while the rest scattered; two others force-landed, with one being declared a complete write-off. One damaged P-400 ditched, but the pilot swam ashore and was helped by Papuan natives and later returned to his unit. B-26s also bombed Buna that morning and reported hitting the aircraft dispersal area.

USAAF bombers were also active over Milne Bay, with eight B-17E/Fs arriving after dawn. The low cloud ceiling forced bombing runs from 1,500ft, but even at this altitude only two of the warships supporting the landing were slightly damaged. Antiaircraft fire accounted for one new B-17F, while another crash-landed at Port Moresby due to battle damage and was scrapped. Efforts later in the day against the invasion force by three 22nd Bomb Group B-26s and another nine B-17s failed to locate the ships through rainstorms and low-hanging overcast, and instead bombed the landing area. Two 3rd Bomb Group B-25Cs also bombed the landing area and reported explosions among the trees.

Concurrent RAAF attacks had greater success against the Japanese landing force. Beginning at around dawn, during the morning B-17 attack, 14 Kittyhawks of Nos 75

Dogfight over Milne Bay

Having been unable, due to adverse weather over Buna the previous day, to launch air support for the Milne Bay invasion force, on August 27 eight 2nd Air Group Vals escorted by seven Tainan and 2nd Air Group Zeros arrived over Milne Bay around 0815hrs and attacked Gurney Strip. After the Japanese bombed and strafed the airfield, the Zeros spotted a B-17 and a few B-26s that had been searching for ship targets below the overcast and chased them but to no effect. As the B-26s escaped westward, two attacking Zeros, hit by ground fire while strafing Gurney, went down in Milne Bay, one of them crashing while the other ditched. Two other Tainan Air Group Zeros attempted to strafe the ditched Zero to sink it to preclude its capture by the Allies. At that moment six No 75 Squadron Kittyhawks returned from a patrol over the east bay. While four Kittyhawks chased the departing Vals, the No 75 Squadron commander and his wingman bounced the two strafing Zeros, which were at an altitude of about 200 ft. The Zeros were surprised and shot down with both pilots killed. Overall, the morning's combat resulted in the loss of four Zeros and two Vals while No 75 Squadron lost one Kittyhawk and pilot, probably shot down by another Zero in combat over the jungle near the airfield.

Troops of the IJN SNLF lie dead along with a destroyed barge at Milne Bay. On August 26, 1942, the two RAAF Kittyhawk squadrons based there played havoc with the landing force, which was left without air cover. Bad weather that day kept six Zeros and eight Vals designated for invasion support grounded at Buna. (NARA)

and 76 Squadrons, along with the sole No 6 Squadron Hudson left at Gurney, attacked the landing site. For over three hours, relays of RAAF fighters – close to 50 sorties in all between the two squadrons – strafed all the equipment sighted on the beach and in the water, also raking the jungle in the hope of hitting troops and any supplies sheltering there. The Kittyhawks destroyed all the barges and almost all the fuel, rations, ammunition, and equipment landed on the beach. That afternoon, No 75 Squadron also conducted its first close air support mission by strafing areas specified by flares or colored smoke to aid the Australian 61st Battalion's counterattack against Japanese positions. The day's heavy strafing ruined the gun barrels of many of the Kittyhawks, and new ones had to be flown in from Townsville by the RAAF No 1 Rescue and Communications Flight.

The morning of August 27 was very busy for both sides. The Japanese renewed the fight when the 25th Air Flotilla mounted a raid in the very early hours against Port Moresby by four bombers that made five passes to bomb through the overcast. Although at least 12 22nd Bomb Group B-26s staged there from Garbutt the previous afternoon, the raid caused no damage. After dawn, it was the Americans' turn, with 14 41st Fighter Squadron P-39Ds/P-400s escorting seven 22nd Bomb Group B-26s to attack Buna. While the escort tangled with six patrolling Tainan Air Group Zeros, the bombers were able to crater the runway and dispersal areas with 135 100lb high explosive bombs dropped from 1,500ft. The escorting fighters claimed five kills for one damaged P-39D written off upon their return, though they actually shot down only one Zero.

This raid failed to catch any aircraft on the ground because the Japanese had already launched a raid against Milne Bay. A total of seven Zeros from both the Tainan and 2nd Air Groups escorted eight Vals, each carrying two 132lb bombs. The Vals became separated from their escort when they descended through the overcast to locate their targets. In the process, they ran into some of the 14 No 76 Squadron Kittyhawks that had been airborne since dawn to renew their strafing attacks against the SNLF troops. The Kittyhawks shot down two Vals after they dropped their bombs at Gurney without damaging the runway. The Zeros finally arrived below the overcast after the Vals attacked and the Kittyhawks had landed, and began strafing Gurney, destroying a 19th Bomb Group LB-30 grounded since delivering 40mm Bofors guns on August 20. Intense antiaircraft fire claimed two Zeros.

The other Zeros climbed away from their attack only to run into ten 22nd Bomb Group B-26s at 1,500ft that had given up after an hour's search for the Japanese ships in the bay and were looking for secondary targets ashore. None of the B-26s were lost in the ensuing action. At this moment, three No 75 Squadron Kittyhawks returned from a patrol at the eastern end of the bay and bounced the Zeros. In the resulting fight, two more Zeros were lost at the cost of one Kittyhawk, whose pilot was killed. Later that day, two No 76 Squadron Kittyhawks were lost to unknown causes while directly supporting Australian troops. One was piloted by the squadron commander – when it was later completed, No 3 strip at Milne Bay was renamed Turnbull in his honor.

The two RAAF squadrons maintained a combined average of 28 airworthy Kittyhawks throughout the battle and continued ground support to the troops on succeeding days. But on the afternoon of August 28, in reaction to the close proximity of Gurney to the Japanese position and because a Japanese attack was expected that night, all the Kittyhawks and pilots were withdrawn to Port Moresby. There they received maintenance each night, returning to Gurney each morning to resume attacks against the SNLF. On August 29, a Japanese convoy with reinforcements for Milne Bay was spotted by a No 6 Squadron Hudson returning from a reconnaissance mission near Rabaul, and was bombed but without effect. Later sorties by the Hudson and six Kittyhawks carrying bombs failed to locate the convoy in the bad weather and fading light. On the same day, the 80th Fighter Squadron sent 17 P-400s to escort five 22nd Bomb Group B-26s targeting Buna. The morning raid encountered only weak antiaircraft fire – the ensuing bombing and strafing destroyed at least three Zeros and two Tainan Air Group Betty transports.

As the RAAF took a mounting toll of Japanese troops and equipment, the IJNAF could only render ineffective support to the Milne Bay force. USAAF attacks on Buna prompted the 25th Air Flotilla to recall all remaining aircraft to Rabaul on August 29, and no further missions were flown from Buna against Milne Bay. On the morning of August 31, the 25th Air Flotilla ordered seven 2nd Air Group Zeros to patrol over the beachhead. The fighters lingered for less than an hour, did not attack the Australians in the air or on the ground, and

On September 1, 1942, the 11th Air Fleet launched a 20-plane force from Rabaul against two Allied vessels resupplying the Milne Bay garrison. Bad weather thwarted the Japanese, and three 2nd Air Group Vals, low on fuel, set down on a nearby beach. Here, natives salvage one Val for Allied intelligence. (NARA)

saw no sign of their own troops hiding in the jungle. Planned raids on Milne Bay launched from Rabaul on September 1 failed due to adverse weather, the second costing three Vals that ran out of fuel and force-landed on the beach. No other IJNAF missions were flown in support of the Milne Bay force. Admitting defeat, the Japanese successfully withdrew the remaining SNLF troops on the night of September 5.

Allied airpower asserts itself: Kokoda and Buna

September marked a pivotal point in the air campaign. Since April, American airpower had operated under virtual RAAF control due to the command arrangements and personnel put in place by then-USAFAI chief Brett. Kenney's formation of separate USAAF and RAAF operational commands under Allied Air Forces and the establishment of Whitehead's ADVON at Port Moresby in August revitalized Allied air efforts. Formal activation of the 5th Air Force on September 3, coupled with increased USAAF staffing and unit organizational reforms, the creation on September 1 of the RAAF's No 9 Operational Group under Group Captain Garing, and the formal designation of RAAF Command, Allied Air Forces under Bostock on September 21, served to clarify command relationships and increase the effectiveness of Allied airpower.

New Allied units were added during this period and "strike" forces took form. Both USAAF and RAAF strike forces were based on new weapons and tactics for twin-engine aircraft, with the goal of attacking the Achilles' heel of the Japanese forces – logistics. The 3rd Bomb Group's 89th Bomb Squadron – equipped with A-20As carrying four extra nose-

Group Captain William "Bull" Garing, left, ran the operations of RAAF No 9 Group, initially headquartered at Milne Bay but later at Port Moresby, from September 1942 to February 1943. An energetic officer operationally in tune with Kenney and Whitehead, he formed the RAAF's twin-engine bombers into an effective "strike group." (Claringbould)

mounted .50-caliber machine guns, racks for 23lb parafrag bomblets, and 450-gallon bomb bay fuel tanks – completed its move to Three Mile 'Drome by September 9. The 43rd Bomb Group's 63rd Bomb Squadron at Mareeba finally received its B-17Fs in August and practiced "skip" bombing from low altitude during August and September. Two squadrons of the 38th Bomb Group's B-25Cs also became operational at Horn Island on September 9. RAAF No 30 (Beaufighter) and No 100 (Beaufort) Squadrons became operational at Milne Bay as of September 6 to form No 9 Group's strike force. Other key additions included the 8th Photo Reconnaissance Squadron moving its F-4As to 14 Mile 'Drome on September 9 and the 49th Fighter Group's 7th Fighter Squadron moving first to 30 Mile 'Drome on September 14, and later to 14 Mile 'Drome. Its sister 8th Fighter Squadron moved in October, followed by the 9th Fighter Squadron in November. Meanwhile, the 8th Fighter Group's 35th and 36th Fighter Squadrons moved to Milne Bay to relieve Nos 75 and 76 Squadrons, which returned to Australia.

Up to this point in the campaign, the Allies had mainly conducted a counter-air strategy focused on attacking Japanese airfields. These efforts achieved some success in blunting the IJNAF air offensive. Concurrent attacks by medium- and high-level bombers against Japanese maritime traffic, in port or at sea, yielded abysmal results. Now, Allied strategy shifted heavily to employing twin-engine bombers, escorted by fighters, in low-altitude bombing and strafing of both land and maritime targets supporting Japanese troops on New Guinea.

This shift in Allied strategy was possible because Japan's Solomons campaign continued to bleed off significant IJNAF airpower, making 11th Air Fleet operations in the New Guinea campaign sporadic. As IJNAF units were decimated in Solomons air battles, Rabaul saw an influx of additional units, many taken from carrier air groups. On August 21, the 6th Air Group arrived in 18 Zeros flown by its most experienced pilots and remained until moving to the Solomons in early October. It was joined by 3rd Air Group Zeros in September, operating out of Rabaul until November 1, while the Kanoya Air Group sent nine Zeros and 23 Bettys on or around September 19. Bettys from the Takao, Chitose, and Misawa Air Groups remained in action. However, the 4th Air Group was withdrawn to Japan in

The P-40E served with the USAAF 49th Fighter Group in the campaign after the unit moved from Darwin to Port Moresby, beginning in September. The P-40E was outperformed by the Zero aerodynamically but could take much more battle damage and still get home. Here, a 7th Fighter Squadron P-40E is rearmed. (NARA)

OPPOSITE THE PAPUAN CAMPAIGN

September for refitting. In mid-September, Vice-Admiral Tsukahara regrouped 11th Air Fleet units into a new command structure comprising the 5th and 6th Attack Forces. All fighters and seaplanes fell under the 5th Attack Force, and all bombers – except those of the Kanoya Air Group – were placed under the 6th Attack Force. Furthermore, as of September 8, the 11th Air Fleet abandoned Buna airstrip when the 2nd Air Group's remaining Zeros withdrew to Lae.

In September, the 11th Air Fleet mounted two major attacks against Port Moresby in support of Operation *RE*. On September 7 and 21, 26 and 36 Zeros, respectively, escorted 27 Bettys in daylight raids against airfields, without opposition from American fighters on either occasion. The September 7 strike by Kisarazu, Chitose, and Misawa Air Group Bettys from 23,000ft on Seven Mile 'Drome cratered the airstrip, taxiway, and dispersal areas, severely damaged two P-400s, and lightly damaged at least two others. However, the September 21 midday mission against the newly completed 30 Mile 'Drome saw the Bettys from the Kisarazu, Kanoya, Chitose, and Misawa Air Groups completely miss the cloud-covered aerodrome from 27,000ft. One Betty, hit by antiaircraft fire on September 7, crash-landed on the north shore of Papua, the only aircraft casualty in either raid. The September 7 mission marked the only time the 6th Air Group's Zeros were active during the campaign, while the September 21 raid was the first flown by Kanoya Air Group Zeros.

Also during this period, the 11th Air Fleet mounted resupply operations for Japanese ground troops. The first occurred on September 23, when eight Misawa Air Group Bettys, escorted by 18 3rd Air Group Zeros, orbited Kokoda for about 20 minutes while dropping supplies to the South Seas Force, which had been cut off from supplies along the trail by flooding of the Kumusi River. Another supply drop by nine unescorted Misawa Air Group Bettys on the afternoon of October 28 was also successful. However, this was practically the extent of IJNAF support to the South Seas Force during the critical period of its retreat from Kokoda toward Buna.

US troops of the 101st Coast Artillery man a Bofors 40mm antiaircraft gun at 14 Mile 'Drome. Because Allied fighters often had difficulty intercepting 11th Air Fleet bombers before they reached their airfield targets, antiaircraft guns became the only defense. They sometimes thwarted attacks and damaged many Japanese aircraft. (NARA)

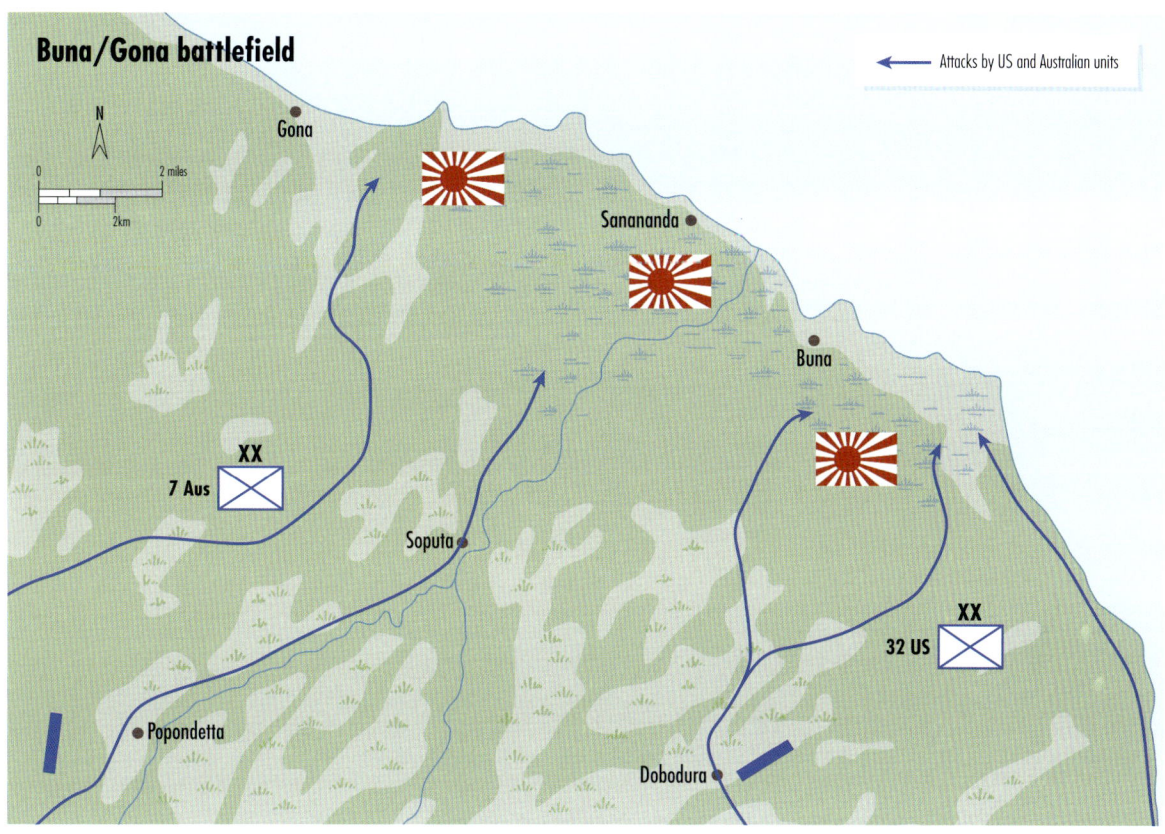

Just as Japanese airpower was being diverted away from New Guinea, some Allied airpower was siphoned off to support the Solomons campaign. Heavy and medium bombers, fighters, reconnaissance, and transport aircraft were at different times devoted to Solomons support missions, or even temporarily held back ("sandbagged" was Kenney's term) while in transit from the US to the SWPA. American commanders in the South Pacific requested that Kenney make hitting Rabaul his top priority, and he complied within his means as such missions also potentially supported SWPA objectives. From September 18 to November 30, Kenney's aircraft flew 180 B-17E/F, 11 Catalina, and two B-24D sorties against Rabaul. For example, Allied raids on Rabaul on September 15 and 16 and October 5, 9, 10, 13, and 23, mostly at night by B-17E/Fs but some by Catalinas, were specifically timed to coincide with American operations or to disrupt Japanese operations in the Solomons. The October 23 mission was notable for the first operational use of skip bombing by the six 63rd Bomb Squadron's B-17E/Fs involved, though they sunk no vessels. Shore installations did receive damage from the six 64th Bomb Squadron B-17E/Fs participating in the attack. Rabaul-area targets were hit at least seven more times between late October and January 17, 1943, with the newly operational 90th Bomb Group's B-24Ds flying their maiden mission of the campaign against Simpson Harbor on the night of November 16–17, picking up where the recently departed 19th Bomb Group left off. However, of the ten B-24Ds on the mission, only two managed to bomb the harbor from 7,000–10,000ft, claiming a hit on a merchant ship. Two others bombed Lakunai and Vunakanau through clouds, with unknown results. One B-24D carrying both the 90th Bomb Group and 320th Bomb Squadron commanders vanished through unknown causes. This, along with one earlier B-24D crash on takeoff and other group miscues, caused Kenney to withdraw the unit temporarily for further training. Kavieng, from which 751 Air Group Bettys conducted periodic nuisance raids against Port Moresby and Milne Bay, also came in for attacks, usually at night by Nos 11 and 20 Squadron Catalinas dropping demolition, incendiary, and fragmentation bombs during armed reconnaissance flights.

A greater share of Allied air missions over the remainder of the campaign were transport/supply, ground support, and maritime interdiction, though counter-air was still pursued. The Allies continued to waste sorties on Buna airstrip as late as December 2, though the Japanese had not used it since September. The Allies also flew periodic bombing attacks against Gasmata, Vunakanau, and Lakunai. But Lae airfield offered the most lucrative target, especially after the IJNAF reinforced it on October 31 with 27 202 and 251 Air Group Zeros, on November 16 with 582 Air Group Zeros and Vals, and on November 20 with about a dozen 252 Air Group Zeros. IJAAF Oscars also operated from Lae, beginning in late December. An example of the attention the Allies paid to Lae occurred on November 22. Though weather was initially poor, one B-17E/F dropped four 500lb bombs during the late morning, destroying some shacks. After the weather cleared somewhat, six Beaufighters strafed and claimed hits on one airborne and four parked Zeros. Later that afternoon, six Beaufighters and nine A-20As strafed several Zeros at the field and fired on three that were airborne, claiming one probably destroyed and another damaged.

Transport and supply missions in support of the Allied New Guinea Force included delivery or airdropping of supplies, medical evacuation, and large-scale deployment of troops. In early September, C-47s of the 21st and 22nd Troop Carrier Squadrons, based at Brisbane and Melbourne, respectively, and Hudsons of RAAF No 32 Squadron, based at Horn Island, were the mainstay of Allied air transport and supply efforts, though a hodgepodge of other military and civilian types were also employed. These were joined by 13 C-47s of 6th Troop Carrier Squadron at Five Mile 'Drome by October 13 and seven 33rd Troop Carrier Squadron C-47s at Brisbane and Cairns in late October, and by No 6 Squadron Hudsons in November. By early November, all Allied transport units, including No 1 Rescue

The 90th Bomb Group's B-24Ds became operational at Iron Range in November. The group arrived that month to share heavy bombardment duties with the 43rd Bomb Group. After serious losses on its initial November 16–17 night mission to Rabaul, the group stood down for retraining and resumed operations in December. (Claringbould)

and Communications Flight (later Squadron), were consolidated at Five Mile 'Drome, while the 374th Troop Carrier Group, which moved from Brisbane to Port Moresby in December, comprised the USAAF units.

During the South Seas Force's push from Buna to Kokoda and beyond between July and September, resupply by air of the defending New Guinea Force had been very difficult. Bad weather, lack of aircraft, uncertainty of the correct drop location due to obscure terrain, and poor packing all greatly limited this effort. The 11th Air Fleet's August 17 air raid on Seven Mile 'Drome destroyed or seriously damaged seven of the valuable C-47s, leaving only one serviceable C-47 available. Until the Japanese captured it on July 29, the Allies used the small airstrip at Kokoda to land supplies that were then carried by hundreds of native bearers along the trail to the front lines, a slow, manpower-intensive method during which the bearers themselves consumed some of the rations being carried. Supplies were also dropped and husbanded at two relatively flat, easily visible dry lake beds in the mountains. Overall, the scale of the air supply effort never fully met the ground force's requirements. Meanwhile, air supply to Kanga Force at Wau used the small airstrip there, which was very challenging for aircraft, usually one per day, to land at due to its significant 12 percent gradient and mountainous surrounding terrain.

Even after the Allies went on the offensive in late September, the Australian 7th Division commander was "gravely concerned" by the supply situation his troops continued to face. Part of the solution to getting more supplies to New Guinea Force was better tactics – dropping from 400–500ft altitude – and better packing of supplies to buffer the impact upon landing. The limited supply of parachutes was used for fragile cargo such as ammunition and medical supplies. The supply problems eased greatly when the Allies recaptured Kokoda and built additional airstrips on the northeastern side of the Owen Stanleys closer to the front. By November, supplies and small-scale reinforcements were being flown the 35 minutes

C-47s and other Allied aircraft flew hundreds of sorties to keep the Allied troops supplied. They delivered almost 5 million pounds of supplies between November 13, 1942 and January 23, 1943 to Dobodura, Pongani, and Popondetta, and via airdrops. Here, C-47s fly over the Owen Stanley Range to Dobodura on December 1, 1942. (MacArthur Memorial)

THE CAMPAIGN

Air transport proved to be the most critical advantage the Allies had in the campaign, hauling troops, supplies, and equipment. Here a B-17E converted for transport duty flew a 105mm howitzer, ammunition, and gun crew from Brisbane to Seven Mile 'Drome on November 15 to support the Buna assault. Later, C-47s flew the guns to the front. General. Kenney inspects the equipment, far right. (NARA)

from Port Moresby to airstrips at Pongani, Dobodura, and Popondetta, including artillery pieces that moved into action within a day of delivery. However, it took placement of US quartermaster personnel at these locations in early December to expedite supply transfer to the field. Overall, from November 13, 1942 to January 23, 1943, the Allies moved almost 5 million pounds of supplies via air drops and deliveries to New Guinea Force.

Troop transport was a successful 5th Air Force innovation in support of ground operations. MacArthur was eager to get US troops forward to support the Australian troops fighting the South Seas Force. The first major air movement of US troops in the war occurred on September 15, when Allied transports flew 230 troops of the US 32nd Infantry Division's 126th Infantry Regiment from Australia to Port Moresby as a test. Between September 18 and 24, using 12 civilian airliners to supplement military aircraft, the division's entire 128th Infantry Regiment was flown to New Guinea, arriving two days ahead of the rest of the 126th Infantry Regiment that had moved by sea. These movements established the template for later operations in New Guinea.

OCTOBER 1942

8TH FIGHTER GROUP
35th & 36th Fighter Sqns, P-400s & P-39D/Fs	Milne Bay
80th Fighter Sqn, P-400s/P-39D/Fs	Port Moresby

35TH FIGHTER GROUP
39th Fighter Sqn, P-400s/P-39D/Fs	Garbutt
40th & 41st Fighter Sqns, P-400s & P-39D/Fs	Milne Bay

49TH FIGHTER GROUP
7th Fighter Sqn, P-40Es	Port Moresby
8th Fighter Sqn, P-40Es	Port Moresby
9th Fighter Sqn, P-40Es	Port Moresby

3RD BOMB GROUP
8th Bomb Sqn, A-20As	Charters Towers
89th Bomb Sqn, A-20As	Port Moresby
13th & 90th Bomb Sqns, B-25Cs	Charters Towers

19TH BOMB GROUP
28th, 30th & 93rd Bomb Sqns, B-17Es	Mareeba
435th Bomb Sqn, B-17Es	Garbutt

22ND BOMB GROUP
2nd & 408th Bomb Sqns, B-26s	Reid River
19th Bomb Sqn, B-26s	Iron Range
33rd Bomb Sqn, B-26s	Iron Range

38TH BOMB GROUP
71st & 405th Bomb Sqns, B-25Cs	Port Moresby

43RD BOMB GROUP
63rd Bomb Sqn, B-17Fs	Mareeba
8th Photo Reconnaissance Sqn, F-4s	Port Moresby
6th Troop Carrier Sqn, C-47	Port Moresby
No 6 Sqn, Hudsons	Horn Island (forward detachment at Milne Bay)
No 1 Rescue & Communications Flight, Ansons/DH-89s/DH-82s	Port Moresby
Nos 11 & 20 Sqns, Catalinas	Bowen
No 100 Sqn, Beauforts	Horn Island (forward detachment at Milne Bay)
No 30 Sqn, Beaufighters	Port Moresby

Rapid air transport of ground units to the front was a trailblazing achievement for the Allies in the campaign. Here, elements of the 32nd Infantry Division prepare to board for the Buna front. This particular 6th Troop Carrier Squadron C-47 was shot down by Zeros near Dobodura on November 26. (Claringbould)

On October 5, the 21st Troop Carrier Squadron flew 60 sorties, unopposed by the Japanese, from 14 Mile 'Drome moving the Australian 2/20th Battalion and American engineers to Wanigela, which was established as a hub for supplies transported by air and by seaborne barges from Milne Bay. The success of this operation, and the concurrent struggle of the 126th Infantry Regiment to move overland toward the same location, convinced MacArthur that the mobility afforded by Kenney's transports was the key to future Allied troop movements. Accordingly, in the first half of November, air transports brought the remainder of the 32nd Infantry Division to Wanigela and Pongani in preparation for the Allied offensive against the Japanese Buna–Sanananda–Gona stronghold.

Ground support missions, which included "close" support against Japanese troops in contact with Allied troops and "direct" support against South Seas Force rear area targets, supplies, and lines of communication, enjoyed a mixed bag of success. Such missions began just after the Japanese landed at Buna and Gona in July. A system set up to allow New Guinea Force to request close air support from 5TH ADVON, usually requiring requests to be submitted by 1700hrs the previous day, worked reasonably well. Over the period of heaviest ground combat from August 26, 1942 to January 2, 1943, Whitehead received 110 requests for close support from New Guinea Force, of which 72 were executed. The remainder were refused due to poor weather, poor target selection, or lack of aircraft availability. Allied ground commanders were lukewarm regarding these missions since they were generally

Japanese strike at Oro Bay

Until the airfield at Dobodura was completed, the US 32nd Infantry Division needed to rely largely on seaborne supplies to prepare for the upcoming assault on Buna. But on November 16, the 11th Air Fleet launched an attack against the recently detected Allied supply activity at Oro Bay. Arriving about 1745hrs, after Allied fighter cover had departed, twelve 582 Air Group Vals attacked three trawlers and one captured Japanese barge as they approached the landing site. All four craft were destroyed, along with heavy weapons, ammunition, rations, radios, and medical supplies. Major General Edwin Harding, the 32nd Infantry Division commander, was aboard one of the trawlers and had to swim to shore with some of his staff after the attack, but 23 US personnel were killed and many others wounded.

A No 22 Squadron Boston exploded in midair on November 29, 1942, while attacking Japanese troop positions near Gona. The unit's Bostons had problems using old British 20lb fragmentation bombs. Originally designed for hand-dropping from open-cockpit aircraft, the slipstream sometimes caused the bombs to hit the fuselage upon release, triggering their impact fuses. (MacArthur Memorial)

ineffectual, and several times inadvertently caused Allied casualties. Target identification by aviators was a major problem throughout the campaign due to dense jungle growth and Japanese camouflage. Various expedients were tried by Allied troops to aid aircraft in hitting a target, including providing map coordinates, using white or reflecting surfaces, flares, smoke, and rocket markers, but maps were too poor and battle lines were often too close, fluid, or disjointed for these to work consistently. Close air support missions were at first conducted by USAAF P-40Es, P-39s/P-400s, and A-20As, the latter employing parafrag bombs. They were joined later by B-25Cs, B-26s, and RAAF Wirraways, Bostons, and Beaufighters. In the majority of cases, the impact of these sorties was impossible to assess; captured Japanese diaries indicated the South Seas Force troops had little concern about them.

The Japanese were much more concerned by Allied attacks against their maritime resupply network, South Seas Force facilities ashore, and along the Buna–Kokoda Trail. Kenney and Whitehead, inspired by the RAAF Milne Bay performance, stepped up Allied air attacks on Japanese supply lines, flying roughly 2,000 sorties from August to November. These Allied direct support missions were somewhat more successful than close air support operations. Kokoda, the Buna–Kokoda Trail, and shore facilities in the Gona–Sanananda–Buna area came under almost daily attack from late August until December from RAAF and USAAF fighters and bombers, and even 30th Bomb Squadron B-17E/Fs staged to 14 Mile 'Drome. Fighters charged with escorting transports carried bombs to conduct ground attacks once their escort duties were concluded. For example, on November 15, just ahead of the planned Allied ground thrust against Buna, two missions were flown by both No 30 Squadron Beaufighters from Five Mile 'Drome and 22nd Bomb Group B-26s – the Beaufighters strafed antiaircraft positions and barges near Buna, while B-26s bombed the same targets. No 22 Squadron Bostons, also flying from Five Mile, made their combat debut that day as well, strafing buildings and barges at Gona.

Another frequent target was the Wairopi Bridge over the Kumusi River between Buna and Kokoda, nestled in a deep valley along the only path the South Seas Force received supplies. USAAF P-39s/P-400s first attacked it unsuccessfully in early August. Operating from 14 Mile

'Drome, the newly arrived 49th Fighter Group's 7th Fighter Squadron flew its first-ever dive-bombing mission against the bridge on September 21, causing it to sag. Thereafter, USAAF and RAAF fighter and bomber attacks forced the Japanese to continuously repair damage until it was completely destroyed around October 18. During this series of attacks, the South Seas Force received fewer supplies despite adding other river crossings. The emaciated condition of its troops and their difficulty in bringing vital equipment across the Kumusi as they retreated in November testified to the effectiveness of the effort.

The Japanese reengaged in Papuan airspace in November as their Solomons effort fizzled and as the Allies recaptured Kokoda and prepared to assault Buna. On November 16, the IJNAF attacked the 32nd Infantry Division's supply boats at Oro Bay as the division positioned for the thrust toward Buna. Six 582 Air Group Zeros and 12 582 Air Group Vals attacked around 1745hrs, after American fighter cover departed for Port Moresby. Bombs destroyed three trawlers and a captured Japanese barge loaded with heavy weapons, ammunition, and rations. The attack forced the unit to be completely dependent on air supply until more sea transport could be acquired.

During November and December, the Japanese mounted several seaborne resupply/reinforcement efforts for Buna, and IJNAF aircraft were often active in covering these convoys. Mirroring their operations in the Solomons, the Japanese shifted to using destroyers for transport operations. Using their high speed and operating primarily at night, these ships were difficult for Allied airpower to counter. Early on November 17, five destroyers carrying 1,000 troops for Buna departed Rabaul. Shrouded by bad weather, the convoy was also covered by three 582 Air Group Zeros from Rabaul that refueled at Lae and returned, while another nine 582 Air Group Zeros flew into Lae that evening. Four destroyers offloaded that night and returned to Rabaul the next day.

Another convoy of three destroyers carrying 500 more troops left Rabaul at midnight on November 18. A combat air patrol (CAP) was provided by eight 582 Air Group Zeros the next morning and an additional six during the afternoon. Making good use of signals intelligence, Kenney and Whitehead mustered a series of attacks on this convoy, though their efforts were hampered by poor weather. Around midday, seven 64th Bomb Squadron B-17Fs bombed the destroyers south of Gasmata, dropping 56 500lb bombs from high altitude over 45 minutes, but with no effect. Two 63rd Bomb Squadron B-17Fs tried again at dusk as the destroyers reached Buna. The heavy bombers beat off attacks by the defending Zeros, destroying one, but their bombing was ineffective. After dark, six 64th Bomb Squadron B-17Fs dropped flares under the 1,000ft cloud base and conducted skip-bombing attacks. This resulted in serious damage to one destroyer, which had to be towed back to Rabaul, and minor damage to another. All the troops were delivered safely.

In a rare event, another convoy of four destroyers transporting 800

Eighteen RAAF No 4 Squadron Wirraways, flying first from 12 Mile 'Drome and later deployed to Dobodura, conducted tactical reconnaissance, artillery spotting, bombing, and strafing in support of the Allied assault on the Gona–Sanananda–Buna enclave. Here, a Wirraway operates over a US 32nd Infantry Division position near Buna. (NARA)

A 49th Fighter Group P-40E with two 300lb bombs for a ground attack mission from 14 Mile 'Drome during the Buna fighting. At the time, American fighters often flew transport escort missions armed with bombs, afterwards attacking Japanese targets on the ground. The 49th flew its first dive-bombing mission on September 21. (Claringbould)

troops of the 21st Mixed Independent Brigade from Rabaul to Buna was successfully attacked by B-17E/Fs of the 43rd Bomb Group on the afternoon of November 29. The attack took place in the Vitiaz Strait; two of the destroyers were badly damaged and the convoy returned to Rabaul without reaching its destination. One B-17F shadowing the convoy after the attack was lost through unknown causes with all 11 aboard.

Allied air attacks against convoys headed to Lae were more effective than the low number of enemy vessels sunk or damaged might indicate. In some cases, the Japanese were able to land troops but did not have time to also unload the needed supplies and equipment. In other cases, the landings were made far from the Buna–Sanananda–Gona front, further delaying the arrival of men and materiel. As an example, another five-destroyer reinforcement convoy was attempted between December 12 and 14. Covered by bad weather along a circuitous route from Rabaul via the Admiralty Islands and with flights of Zeros, it endured two bombings late on December 13 without suffering any damage. However, the destroyers disembarked their loads overnight on December 13–14 near the mouth of the Mambare River, about 50 miles northwest of the front, due to the threat of Allied airpower. To help offset the seaborne resupply problems, the 11th Air Fleet mounted a last-ditch air resupply mission on December 10 with seven 705 Air Group Bettys escorted by 15 Zeros. Some 125 packages were dropped over Buna, with no aircraft losses.

Several Japanese air attacks were mounted in November and December against Allied forces assaulting Buna, Gona, and Sanananda. Most were ineffective, but the November 26 attack featured four 582 Air Group Vals escorted by six 582 Air Group and six 252 Air Group Zeros targeted against Dobodura and Allied coastal supply activity. Although several 49th Fighter Group P-40Es tangled with the attackers and shot down one 582 Air Group fighter, the Zeros still managed to strafe and destroy a trawler grounded on a sand bar, while bombs damaged a C-47 at the airstrip. The 252 Air Group Zeros also shot down two C-47s that had just left Dobodura, killing their crews.

In late December, IJAAF fighters participated in attacks over eastern New Guinea. Around midday on December 27, at least 12 11th Regiment Oscars, escorting four 582 Air Group Vals from Lae, joined 12 582 Air Group Vals – each carrying their usual payload of a 551lb bomb – and 12 582 Air Group Zeros from Rabaul to attack the Buna area. Twelve 39th Fighter Squadron P-38Fs, based at 14 Mile 'Drome and seeing their first air combat in the

Several 39th Fighter Squadron P-38Fs line the runway at 14 Mile 'Drome ready to scramble. Though operational in November, the squadron's first major battle of the New Guinea campaign with P-38s did not come until December 27. Thereafter, the unit tilted the air combat balance in favor of the Allies. (NARA)

campaign, spotted the Japanese formation over the coast and dove to break up the attack. However, two 49th Fighter Group P-40Es which joined the fight were fired on by the P-38Fs, which mistook them for Oscars. The Vals failed to reach their target; one Oscar was shot down and a Val was written off after landing. In return, the Japanese shot down no Allied aircraft, but one heavily damaged P-38F crash-landed at Dobodura.

Allied transports save Wau

Though forced on the defensive after the loss of Buna, the IJA was determined to hold Lae and Salamaua as the western bulwark to the approaches to Rabaul. The Allies maintained Kanga Force at Wau, only 40 miles southwest of Lae, and the Japanese faced the prospect that their forward positions on New Guinea would become untenable.

General Imamura, commanding Japanese troops in New Guinea, advocated an aggressive strategy of reinforcing Lae and then attacking the emerging Allied threat at Wau. The force selected to reinforce Lae was the 51st Division, located at Rabaul. Some 6,000 men were slated for movement, but such a large force could only be moved by convoy. In addition, SNLF troops were selected to reinforce Lae. Getting these reinforcements to their destination required a large convoy of five transports with a strong destroyer escort. Although the convoy was attacked from January 5–8, the Allies were only able to sink two out of the five transports. A variety of aircraft were used, including heavy and medium bombers, with P-38Fs providing

Allied air attack on a Buna resupply convoy

The Japanese undertook many supply runs to the Buna garrison by sea. On December 12, five destroyers carrying an infantry battalion, support troops, and supplies left Rabaul for Buna under cover of bad weather and taking a circuitous route around western New Britain to minimize the threat of Allied detection. But on December 13, the convoy was located and endured three attacks. One of these occurred at 1750hrs when three 43rd Bomb Group B-17Fs found the convoy and dropped 24 500lb bombs on it without effect. The bombers were chased away by a patrol of 582 Air Group Zeros assigned to cover the convoy, but neither side suffered a loss. The attacks did, however, induce the convoy to unload near the mouth of the Mambare River, about 50 miles from the Buna garrison.

From September onward, the 5th Air Force's C-47s became central to the Allies' ground force mobility and combat sustainment in contesting New Guinea. To protect these valuable and scarce assets, fighters usually provided round-trip escort. Here, 35th Fighter Group P-39s escort 6th Troop Carrier Squadron C-47s en route to Wau. (NARA)

cover. When the convoy reached Lae on January 8, it was attacked by 80 Allied aircraft. Zeros and Oscars defended the convoy well. Because most of the personnel and their equipment got through, the Japanese were able to move against Wau with a brigade-sized force in mid-January.

In response, between January 14 and 24, 374th Troop Carrier Group transports flew a battalion of the Australian 17th Brigade into Wau to join Kanga Force. Bad weather delayed further flights until January 29, when additional troops of two additional battalions were flown in over two days to repulse the Japanese attempt to take Wau airfield that had begun on January 27. The transports, escorted by fighters of the 35th and 49th Fighter Groups, flew 244 sorties from January 29 to February 1. Nos 22 and 30 Squadrons were active attacking Japanese positions with bombs and cannon fire. Only on February 6, after Japanese troops had retreated, did the IJAAF make an appearance to prevent any counterattack toward Lae. Late that morning, 29 11th Regiment Oscars escorted at least nine 45th Regiment Lilys to bomb the airstrip, where several C-47s were delivering supplies. A C-47 and a No 4 Squadron Wirraway were destroyed when a stick of bombs hit the center of the runway. Eight 35th Fighter Group P-39s/P-400s escorting five C-47s to Wau became involved in a dogfight with the Oscars. Over the next two hours, all three 35th Fighter Group squadrons and two 49th Fighter Group squadrons participated in a running fight in which the Americans claimed 22 "Zeros"(Oscars) and three Lilys. Additionally, antiaircraft fire at Wau claimed one bomber and two fighters. As usual, these claims were inflated – actual Japanese losses were one Lily and four Oscars. Not just the Americans exaggerated their success – the IJAAF claimed 12 enemy fighters, but not a single American aircraft was lost. This was the only major air battle in February.

Prelude to the battle of the Bismarck Sea

The setback at Wau made the Japanese even more determined to bolster their forward bases on the Huon Gulf. Getting most of the early January convoy through to Lae was considered a success by the Japanese. They took away the lesson that convoys could get through with acceptable losses if the operation was planned and executed carefully.

For the March iteration, the plan was much the same as that used for the January reinforcement convoy. Aircraft based on Rabaul would conduct raids on Allied airfields within range of the convoy's route to neutralize enemy airpower. The only attempt to reduce Allied air capabilities was made on the night of February 20, when seven 751 Air Group Bettys raided Buna. The attack was totally ineffective. A heavy CAP was planned to cover the convoy. The 253 Air Group moved to Gasmata for the convoy operation and the fighter unit from light carrier *Zuiho* was forward-staged from Truk to Kavieng. The timing of the movement was critical – it was decided to wait until a weather front moved into the area to shield the convoy from detection and attack.

To move the desired number of men, a large convoy was assembled. Eight transports were allocated, with seven controlled by the IJA and one by the IJN. Six of the IJA transports were loaded with 6,000 men of the 51st Division and other support units. These ships were loaded in such a manner that separated supplies and units; thus, if any one ship was lost, an entire unit would not be eliminated or all of a vital type of equipment lost. A seventh transport carried aviation fuel in drums. The single IJN ship carried SNLF troops and food for the current garrison.

Escorting the convoy were eight destroyers of the 3rd Destroyer Squadron under the command of Admiral Kimura. All the destroyers were veterans of numerous supply missions to Guadalcanal, and some had conducted supply runs in New Guinea waters. Japanese destroyers were excellent torpedo platforms but lacked sufficient antiaircraft weaponry. However, destroyers were fast and maneuverable, making them very difficult targets to hit from the air, especially from high-altitude bombing. The merchant ships in the convoy were neither well-armed nor maneuverable, making them vulnerable to air attack.

The destruction of the March Lae convoy

Unknown to the Japanese, the seeds of their defeat were already planted. Not only had the Allies developed new tactics and deployed additional aircraft since the January convoy to Lae, but signals intelligence gave them advance warning of the March convoy. By February 16, Allied codebreakers had discerned that a Lae convoy was scheduled for early March. Kenney flew to Port Moresby on February 26 to work on a detailed plan with Whitehead to destroy the convoy. They developed the sequence for a coordinated blow by USAAF heavy and medium bombers, combined with RAAF Beaufighters and Beauforts. To maintain the strength of the bomber squadrons, Kenney temporarily stopped attacks against Rabaul. On February 28, a rehearsal for the coordinated strike was conducted near Port Moresby. During the last week of February, increased reconnaissance over the Bismarck Sea began.

Kimura's convoy departed Rabaul very late on February 28 under the cover of a weather front and headed west along the northern coast of New Britain. Kenney and Whitehead had already surmised that the most likely time for the Japanese to mount the convoy operation was during a period of bad weather. The next day, March 1, the weather continued to be poor, but Kimura's hope that his charges would still be shielded by weather was soon dashed, a B-24D from the 321st Bomb Squadron spotting the convoy at 1500hrs. Only 14 of the 16 ships were sighted, but it was clear that a major Japanese effort was underway. A relief B-24D was unable to regain contact, and eight B-17s sent to launch an attack all failed to spot the convoy later in the day.

On March 2, the convoy was relocated at 0815hrs by another B-24D from the 320th Bomb Squadron. As planned by Kenney and Whitehead, the convoy was attacked by heavy bombers as soon as it was within range. Two waves of bombers were formed, with fighter cover to be provided by two squadrons of P-38Fs. However, the 9th Fighter Squadron missed the rendezvous and did not head to the target area.

The battle of the Bismarck Sea

The culmination of the development of Allied airpower during the campaign was the near total destruction of a major Japanese convoy bound for Lae from Rabaul between February 28 and March 4.

Japanese forces 🔴
- **a** 18 Zeros from 253 Air Group
- **b** 14 Zeros from 204 Air Group
- **c** 27 Oscars from 11th *Sentai*
- **d** 14 Zeros from 253 Air Group
- **e** 12 Zeros from 204 Air Group
- **f** 15 Zeros from *Zuiho*
- **g** 8 Zeros from 252 Air Group

Allied forces 🔵

A
- **First heavy bomber wave, March 2** (14 B-17s from 63rd and 65th Bombardment Squadrons)
- **Second heavy bomber wave, March 2** (11 B-17s from 64th Bombardment Squadron and two B-24s from 321st Bombardment Squadron)
- **Third heavy bomber wave, March 2** (ten B-17s from 64th and 403rd Bombardment Squadrons, one B-24 from 320th Bombardment Squadron)

B 28 P-38s from 9th and 39th Fighter Squadrons

C
- **March 3 morning attack group** (nine B-17s from 64th and 403rd Bombardment Groups, 12 Beaufighters from No 30 Squadron, 12 A-20s from 89th Bombardment Squadron, 12 B-25C-1s from 90th Bombardment, 19 B-25s from 13th, 71st, and 405th Bombardment Squadrons, and ten second-wave B-17s from 63rd and 65th Bombardment Squadrons)
- **March 3 afternoon attack group** (eight B-25C-1s, 19 other B-25s, 15 B-17s)
- **March 4 attack group** (nine B-25C-1s and three B-17s)

EVENTS

1. February 28, 2300hrs. Convoy departs Simpson Harbor.
2. March 1, 1500hrs. Convoy is spotted by a B-24.
3. March 2, 0730–0800hrs. 18 Zeros from 253 Air Group from Kavieng arrive over convoy.
4. 0926hrs. Six B-17s from 65th Bombardment Squadron clash with escorting Zeros.
5. About 0930hrs. Eight B-17s from 63rd Bombardment Squadron make first bombing runs; two hits and some near misses are scored on *Kyokusei Maru*, which sinks within an hour.
6. 0940hrs. 14 Zeros from 204 Air Group reinforce CAP.
7. About 1000hrs. 11 B-17s from 64th Bombardment Squadron and two B-24s from 321st Bombardment Squadron claim a hit on one transport and near miss on another. *Teiyo Maru* takes a direct hit but suffers minimal damage. *Kembu Maru* is near missed. Several B-17s are damaged and two Zeros are lost.
8. Destroyers *Yukikaze* and *Asagumo* deliver survivors from *Kyokusei Maru* to Lae and return to the convoy the next morning.
9. Afternoon. 27 Oscars from 11th *Sentai* arrive in two groups. Ten B-17s and one B-24 attack, but only gain a near miss on *Nojima*. Oscars intercept, but neither side suffers losses.

March 3

10. 0545hrs. B-17s relieve an RAAF Catalina and continue to track convoy.
11. 0600–0800hrs. 41 Zeros arrive over convoy (14 from 253 Air Group from Gasmata, 12 from 204 Air Group from Rabaul, 15 *Zuiho* fighters from Kavieng).
12. 0800hrs. Allied aircraft take off from Port Moresby airfields and rendezvous near Cape Ward Hunt (halfway between Buna and Salamaua).
13. 1000–1030hrs. In a coordinated attack, heavy bombers, Beaufighters, A-20s, and B-25s sink merchants *Kembu Maru* and *Shinai Maru*; all the other transports are crippled. Destroyer *Shirayuki* is sunk; *Arashio* and *Tokitsukaze* are also crippled.
14. After 1030hrs. Four destroyers pick up survivors and head out of the battle area.
15. 1250hrs. Eight Zeros from 252 Air Group arrive over convoy.
16. 1500hrs. The afternoon attack group sinks destroyer *Asashio* and four crippled transports; by the end of the attack, only *Arashio*, *Tokitsukaze*, and transport *Oigawa Maru* are still afloat. Orders are given to strafe Japanese survivors in the water.
17. 2332hrs. PT boats sink *Oigawa Maru*.

March 4

18. *Arashio* sinks in the morning and *Tokitsukaze* is finished off in the afternoon. Japanese survivors in the water are strafed.

The 90th Bomb Squadron's B-25Cs were modified and trained at Kenney's direction as "commerce destroyers." In this capacity, the unit became available for action at the very end of 1942 and was a major participant against the Lae resupply convoy the Allies targeted in the Bismarck Sea in early March 1943. (Claringbould)

By the time the first B-17E/Fs arrived, there was already a strong CAP of Zeros from the 253 Air Group over the convoy. Ranged against the convoy and its CAP was a force of 27 heavy bombers and a single squadron of escorting P-38Fs. The air battle opened with Zeros clashing with six B-17s from the 65th Bomb Squadron. As usual, the Zeros did not press their attacks against the heavily armed B-17s.

First to drop their bombs were the eight B-17s from the 63rd Bomb Squadron. Attacking from a low altitude of 6,500ft, the first wave of bombers claimed two hits and a near miss on a transport. Zeros attacked the B-17s and inflicted damage to four of the bombers. Next to drop were the six B-17s of the 65th Bomb Squadron, which claimed another hit on a different transport. About 30 minutes later, the second wave of 11 B-17s from the 64th Bomb Squadron and two B-24Ds from the 321st came in at 5,000ft. Japanese fighters engaged this group but only succeeded in damaging three bombers. The B-17s claimed another two transport hits or near misses. When the bombers departed, a total of four transports were seen to be on fire and sinking.

Usually, claims from the heavy bomber crews were wildly exaggerated, but not on this occasion. The transport *Kyokusei Maru* was hit twice by bombs, and one crewmember and 485 troops were killed. Since the ship took about an hour to sink, the destroyers *Yukikaze* and *Asagumo* managed to pick up 950 men from the water and headed to Lae. These were the only men destined to reach their destination in any sort of order. Both destroyers returned to the convoy by the morning of March 3. In addition to the sunk transport, the *Teiyo Maru* suffered a direct hit but incurred only minimal damage, while *Kembu Maru* suffered a near miss. No bombers were lost in the attack, while two Zeros were shot down.

Responsibility for protecting the convoy in the afternoon was assigned to the 11th Regiment, which launched 27 Oscars in two groups to provide CAP. A second group of heavy bombers made an afternoon attack with ten B-17s from the 64th and 403rd Bomb Squadrons and one B-24 from the 320th. The defending Oscars managed to damage four of the big bombers and harried the Americans enough so that the only damage was caused by a near miss to the transport *Nojima*.

The heavy bomber attack on March 2 brought an unexpected level of success. However, there was no question of Kimura turning back, even though the weight of air attacks was certain to increase the next day. The convoy passed by the Dampier Strait and then headed through the Vitiaz Strait that night, shadowed by an RAAF Catalina from No 11 Squadron. Having entered the Solomon Sea, it was only some 80nm from Lae.

On March 3, with all his aircraft within range, Kenney could execute his coordinated strike. Kenney's plan called for more attacks by heavy bombers, delivering their bombs from 5,000–6,000ft. B-25s and A-20s from the 3rd and 38th Bomb Groups would attack from two altitudes. Those converted for low-level attacks were ordered to approach their targets at 500ft – those not converted would attack at 5,000–6,000ft. The RAAF was well represented with Beaufighters from No 30 Squadron and Beauforts from No 100 Squadron. Covering the assault force were P-38s.

The Japanese mounted a heavy morning CAP of 41 Zeros. Crucially, these were ordered to fly at medium altitude to intercept the horizontal-attack bombers like those encountered the day before. The Japanese were unaware of the new Allied tactic to attack from low altitude.

Before dawn, a B-17 relieved the Catalina which had been tracking the convoy during the night. The B-17 recorded the return of the two destroyers. Weather over the battle area was not a major factor, with only scattered clouds present.

About 1000hrs on March 3, 1943, a No 30 Squadron Beaufighter records two 90th Bomb Squadron B-25Cs attacking a transport in the Bismarck Sea. Two bomb explosions register hits either on the transport or close alongside, while strafing misses splash on the far side of the transport. (MacArthur Memorial)

Once the Lae resupply convoy was dispersed, the slow merchant ships were even more vulnerable to attack. Here, two 90th Bomb Squadron B-25Cs attack a transport. Their preferred tactic was to attack in pairs, with one B-25 providing suppressive fire against the ship's antiaircraft defenses while the second bombed the target. (USAF)

Before the arrival of Kenney's main attack force, the first assault against Kimura's convoy had already been conducted. Eight Beauforts launched from Milne Bay before dawn, but due to poor weather en route only two made a torpedo run when they arrived in the area of the convoy at first light. Just a single aircraft was able to actually launch its torpedo, but it missed.

After rendezvousing off Cape Ward Hunt, the main attack force headed to its target. Just before 1000hrs, the Japanese spotted the approaching aircraft. The Japanese expected the traditional medium- and high-level bombing attacks, combined with traditional low-level torpedo attacks. They were unprepared for what followed.

Covered by 28 P-38Fs from the 9th and 39th Fighter Squadrons, nine B-17s attacked first. Heavy frontal attacks by the Zeros were unsuccessful, but the bombers failed to score any hits. However, the high-level attack forced the convoy to disperse, making the ships vulnerable to follow-up attacks. As the heavy bombers attacked, 12 Beaufighters from No 30 Squadron approached the convoy at mast-top level at 220kts. The Japanese ships turned towards the approaching aircraft, expecting a torpedo attack. Instead, the Beaufighters swept the decks of the transports with their 20mm cannons and .30-caliber machine guns. Next, 12 A-20As from the 89th Bomb Squadron conducted skip-bombing attacks, each aircraft carrying two 500lb bombs. The effect was immediate – ten hits and two near misses were claimed on seven transports. Even more effective were strafing and masthead bombing attacks by 12 B-25Cs from the 90th Bomb Squadron converted and trained for low-level attack. Each bomber carried three or four 500lb bombs. The protecting Zeros failed to intervene in time and antiaircraft fire was ineffective, leaving the B-25s unhindered to do their deadly work.

Attacking in pairs at 500ft, each pair picked out a ship for attack. Thinking that any aircraft attacking from this height carried torpedoes, they turned toward the attackers to minimize exposure to a torpedo, but this was exactly what the Americans hoped for and expected. The B-25s opened up with their eight .50-caliber machine guns, laying waste to the troops on the weather decks. Once near the target, each bomber released two 500lb bombs that skipped on the water toward their target. Each had a five-second delay to allow the attacking aircraft to escape damage from the resulting explosions and for the bombs to penetrate deep inside the ship before exploding. Even if the bomb missed, it could explode alongside the ship, with a mining effect. The B-25 crews claimed hits on four transport and three destroyers. Of the 37 bombs dropped, crews reported 17 direct hits; a post-attack analysis indicated that 27 of the first 37 bombs hit.

Next up were six B-25s from the 405th Bomb Squadron. Though they were not modified for low-level attacks, the aircrews elected to make them anyway. These B-25s claimed four hits. Seven more B-25s from the 71st Bomb Squadron dropped their weapons from 5,300ft, and 13 from the 13th Bomb Squadron followed from 3,000 and 6,000ft. As the B-25s attacked, ten more B-17s dropped their bombs from higher altitudes. The first group of B-25s was not attacked by Zeros, but the other groups were. The Zeros shot down one B-17 and proceeded to shoot at the surviving crewmembers in their parachutes. None of the attacking high-level bombers recorded a hit, but by this time the convoy had lost all cohesion. In accordance with Japanese doctrine, transports and destroyers maneuvered independently, instead of maintaining formation to provide a greater volume of fire. After making their initial attacks, the Beaufighters, A-20s, and B-25s carried out multiple strafing runs.

As the bombers ravaged the disorganized convoy, an air battle raged above. The CAP concentrated on the heavy bombers and the covering P-38s. Zeros shot down three P-38s from the 39th Fighter Squadron; in return, two Zeros from *Zuiho* were lost. Most importantly, the P-38s prevented the Zeros from inflicting significant losses on the bombers. Only two were lost – the B-17 already mentioned and a B-25 that was attacked on its return trip and forced to make a crash-landing. None of the low-level attackers were lost, due to the ineffectiveness of Japanese antiaircraft fire and the surprise value of the new tactics.

In just 30 minutes, the convoy was shattered. By the end of the morning attack, two transports were sunk and five crippled. With its cargo of aviation fuel, the *Kembu Maru* exploded early on in the attack, probably as a result of strafing. Surprisingly, only 20 Imperial Army soldiers were lost. By 1005hrs, the *Aiyo Maru* was crippled, with 45 of its crew and 278 soldiers lost. Minutes later, the *Shinai Maru*, *Taimei Maru*, and *Teiyo Maru* came under attack, each being hit by at least four bombs. The *Shinai Maru* went down with 18 crew, 45 antiaircraft gunners, and an unknown number of soldiers. Later in the day, the *Taimei Maru* sank with the loss of 44 crew and 35 soldiers. The *Teiyo Maru* experienced the worst loss of life, with 17 crew, 15 gunners, and 1,882 soldiers being killed. The *Oigawa Maru* was hit and brought to a halt. This constituted one of the most devastating air attacks against surface ships during the entire war.

Transport *Kembu Maru* burns on March 3, 1943, after being strafed, initially by RAAF Beaufighters and later by USAAF low-level bombers. The 953-ton IJA transport was carrying 1,000 drums of aviation fuel and 650 drums of other fuel. Shortly afterward, the ship exploded and sank, with the loss of 20 crewmen. (MacArthur Memorial)

Three of eight destroyers were sunk or left sinking after the first attacks. The *Arashio* was struck by three bomb hits, lost all control, and collided with the *Nojima*. The *Shirayuki* was also strafed and hit by a bomb that blew off its stern. Among those wounded by strafing was Admiral Kimura. The *Shikinami* came alongside to save the majority of the crew, but 32 went down with the ship. Kimura was saved and continued to assert control of the battle. The *Tokitsukaze* was attacked by a pair of B-25s. Hit by several bombs, including one in its machinery spaces, the ship was left dead in the water. The *Yukikaze* came alongside to rescue most of the crew (only 19 were lost) and Lieutenant General Adachi Hatazo, commander of the 18th Army. A small damage control party was left on board in an attempt to save the ship.

At the conclusion of the first round of air attacks, Japanese destroyers began rescue operations. Some 2,700 men were saved by four destroyers; once loaded, they retired back up the Vitiaz Strait. A fifth undamaged destroyer, the *Asashio*, stayed behind, hoping to tow the crippled *Arashio* to safety.

After returning to their airfields, Allied aircraft were speedily refueled and rearmed. By 1300hrs, they were heading back to the scene of the morning's slaughter. Due to bad weather over the Owen Stanleys, the Beaufighters and 3rd Bomb Group A-20As were forced to turn back. By this time, 14 Oscars from the 11th Regiment were providing cover. However, they were noted by Allied airmen as lacking aggression.

Just after 1500hrs, the air attacks began anew on the six ships still afloat. Among the attackers were eight B-25Cs from the 90th Bomb Squadron, three other B-25 squadrons, three B-17 squadrons from the 43rd Bombardment Group, and five Bostons from No 22 Squadron. Cover was provided by 18 P-38Fs.

In the absence of effective CAP and facing sporadic antiaircraft fire, the 27 B-25s, 15 B-17s, and five Bostons methodically selected their targets and made careful bomb runs. The skip-bombers from the 90th Bomb Squadron claimed four hits on two destroyers, probably the *Arashio* and *Asashio*. The latter was sunk in the afternoon attack at about 1510hrs after being struck by between four and six direct hits, going down within 15 minutes with all hands. The Allies also claimed hits on two transports. Nineteen other B-25s attacked from various altitudes, some as low as 100ft, and claimed another ten hits. The five Bostons reported attacking a destroyer. The B-17s began their attack at 1512hrs – two

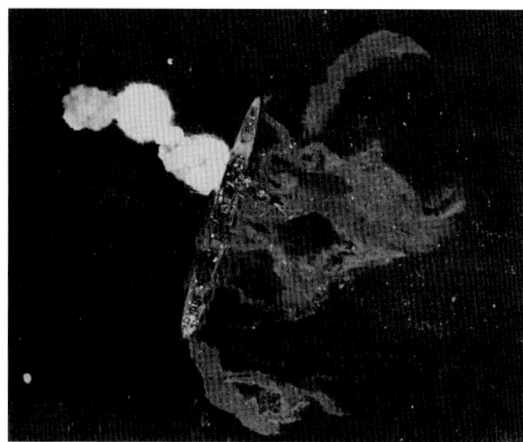

The last two destroyers to be sunk in the Bismarck Sea action were the *Arashio* and *Tokitsukaze*. The former was an Asashio-class unit and the latter a Kagero-class ship. Since both classes were virtually identical, this stricken destroyer surrounded by oil could be either. Both were eventually sunk by low-level attack. (USAF)

hits were claimed on a destroyer. This was possible, since the *Arashio* and *Tokitsukaze* were both stationary targets. By the end of the afternoon attacks, the *Arashio*, *Tokitsukaze*, and *Oigawa Maru* were all drifting without power. That night, ten US Navy motor torpedo boats were dispatched to the area to finish off any cripples. Two of the boats found the *Oigawa Maru* and hit it with two torpedoes. The final transport sank at 2332hrs on March 3, the *Oigawa Maru* taking very heavy losses with 78 crew and 1,151 soldiers killed.

That night, the Japanese mounted rescue operations for the thousands of sailors and soldiers left in the water. Destroyers *Shikinami*, *Asagumo*, and *Yukikaze* unloaded their survivors onto a destroyer from Rabaul sent to meet them, then headed back to the scene to rescue more men. Most of the crew of the *Arashio* (176 men) and all but 19 from *Tokitsukaze* were rescued. The former sank from its damage before dawn on March 4. The *Tokitsukaze* remained afloat until nine B-25Cs sank it during the afternoon.

Even before the last ship was dispatched, there were an enormous number of survivors in the water or on a variety of lifeboats and landing craft from the sunken ships. Beginning on the afternoon of March 3, and throughout the next two days, Allied aircrews were ordered to strafe survivors in the water. In the context of a brutal war, the urge to ensure their destruction before they could get ashore was understandable, but it should be noted that such action was illegal under existing international law. Nevertheless, the aircrews, joined by PT boats, carried out this grisly and unpleasant task. Only a few hundred Japanese reached New Guinea, and they were without weapons or equipment. Between March 3 and 5, Japanese submarines *I-17* and *I-26* picked up 275 soldiers, and on March 7 the submarine *Ro-101* rescued the *Nojima*'s skipper and another 44 soldiers.

Once the rescue operations were over and the Solomon Sea swept clear of Japanese ships, the scope of the Japanese disaster came into focus. Allied aviators accounted for 12 ships – all eight transports and four of the eight destroyers. At least 2,890 men were lost – 2,300 IJA soldiers, 150 SNLF men, 250 destroyer crewmen, and 190 crewmen from the transports. Destruction of an entire Japanese convoy was a turning point in the New Guinea campaign, making a Japanese defense of Lae impossible and future attempts to defend key points along the coast much more difficult.

In the wake of the Bismarck Sea debacle, the Japanese tried to hit back at the Allies in Papua. Between March 9 and 28, Wau, Dobodura, and wharfs in Oro Bay and Porlock Harbor were attacked by relatively large formations of bombers and escorting fighters, but little damage was caused, in the air or on the ground, for the loss of several attacking aircraft. The Allies thereafter gained a two-week respite.

I-Go

The largest IJNAF operation in the South Pacific has been largely forgotten, probably because it was so brief and ineffective. Yamamoto wanted to regain the initiative in the region and delay the start of any Allied offensive. To accomplish these ambitious objectives, he ordered the Combined Fleet's four carriers at Truk to deploy their air groups to Rabaul. Once completed, Yamamoto had over 350 aircraft at his disposal.

Though large, this force was not as powerful as it appeared. By April 1943, the aviators based at Rabaul and Kavieng were no longer in full fighting condition. Disease was taking a toll, leading to poor morale. The skill level of the remaining aviators was low due to heavy losses of more experienced aircrew. To reduce losses, the Bettys were ordered to conduct only high-level attacks, thus reducing their accuracy. Another factor reducing the power of the planned strikes on New Guinea was that the Vals were forced to carry drop tanks to reach their targets instead of their usual 551lb centerline bomb. Consequently, only one 132lb bomb could be carried under each wing, which had little impact on shipping.

With this force, Yamamoto and his staff planned to conduct one strike against shipping off Guadalcanal and three strikes against targets in New Guinea. Designated *I-Go* (Operation "*A*"), all four strikes were planned to occur between April 5 and 20, with the actual timing being dictated by the weather.

The first *I-Go* strike against a target in New Guinea was ordered for April 11. Its objective was to strike shipping in Oro Bay, despite the fact that the amount of shipping present was insignificant. This was the only strike during the operation to be conducted solely by carrier aircraft. A force of 93 aircraft – 72 Zeros and 21 dive-bombers – was committed. The Japanese ran into a large force of P-38Fs on patrol. In addition, another eight P-38s and 30 P-40s (including two RAAF fighters) were scrambled. Both the P-38s and P-40s claimed Vals, but only three were lost. The dive-bombers made their attacks, but with their puny 132lb bombs were only able to damage two small cargo ships and an Australian corvette. In fighter combat of just over 30 minutes, two Zeros were also shot down. Amazingly, despite the large number of Zeros involved, no Allied aircraft were lost.

The following day, Yamamoto unleashed his eagles against airfields around Port Moresby. This was the only *I-Go* attack to target airfields. A total of 188 aircraft were involved, coming from two bomber and four fighter bases. Preceding the strike were two IJNAF Dinah reconnaissance aircraft. Fifty-six Zeros comprised the advance fighter force. The main strike was composed of 54 Bettys covered by another 76 Zeros.

After the Oro Bay strike on shipping, Kenney incorrectly assessed that the next strike would target shipping at Milne Bay. To cope with this blow, he pulled fighters from around Port Moresby and deployed them to Dobodura, to reach Milne Bay more easily.

The first Japanese aircraft took off from Kavieng before dawn; a rendezvous with the elements departing from the Rabaul area was made some two hours later. Approaching at 22,000ft, the huge Japanese formation was detected by radar more than 30 minutes before reaching its target. Beginning at 0930hrs, 74 American fighters were scrambled from three bases. Initial air combat commenced at 1015hrs, with the outnumbered Americans unable to inflict losses on the bombers. The Bettys proceeded to bomb four airfields and the harbor area at Port Moresby. They hit no ships, but destroyed six aircraft on the ground (three Beaufighters and three B-25s) and damaged many others.

Zeros of the 11th Air Fleet prepare for takeoff on an *I-Go* mission. Though Yamamoto gathered significant numbers of aircraft for this multi-mission effort, they achieved very little. However, Yamamoto was misled by the extravagant claims of his aircrews into thinking he had achieved a great victory. (Claringbould)

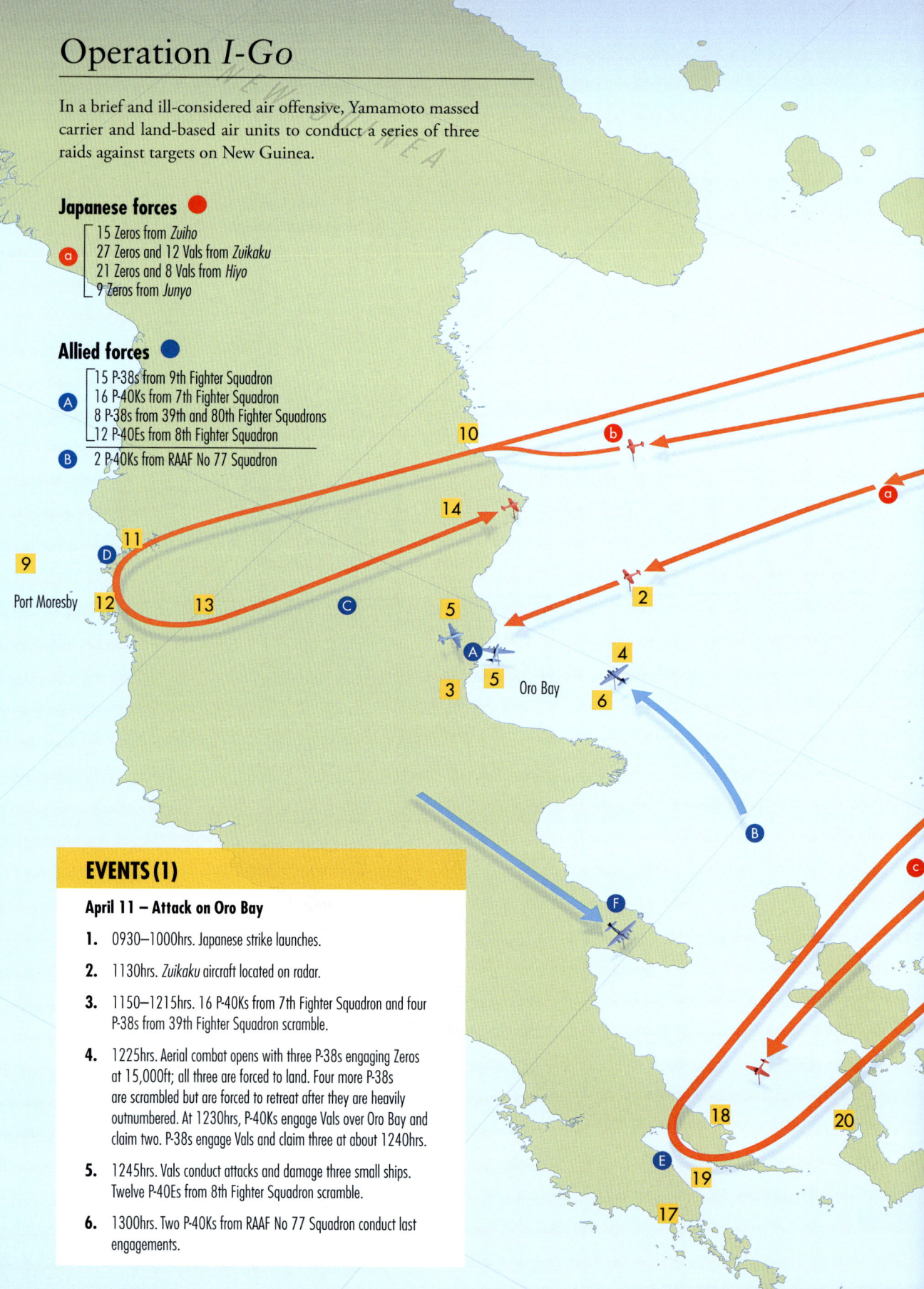

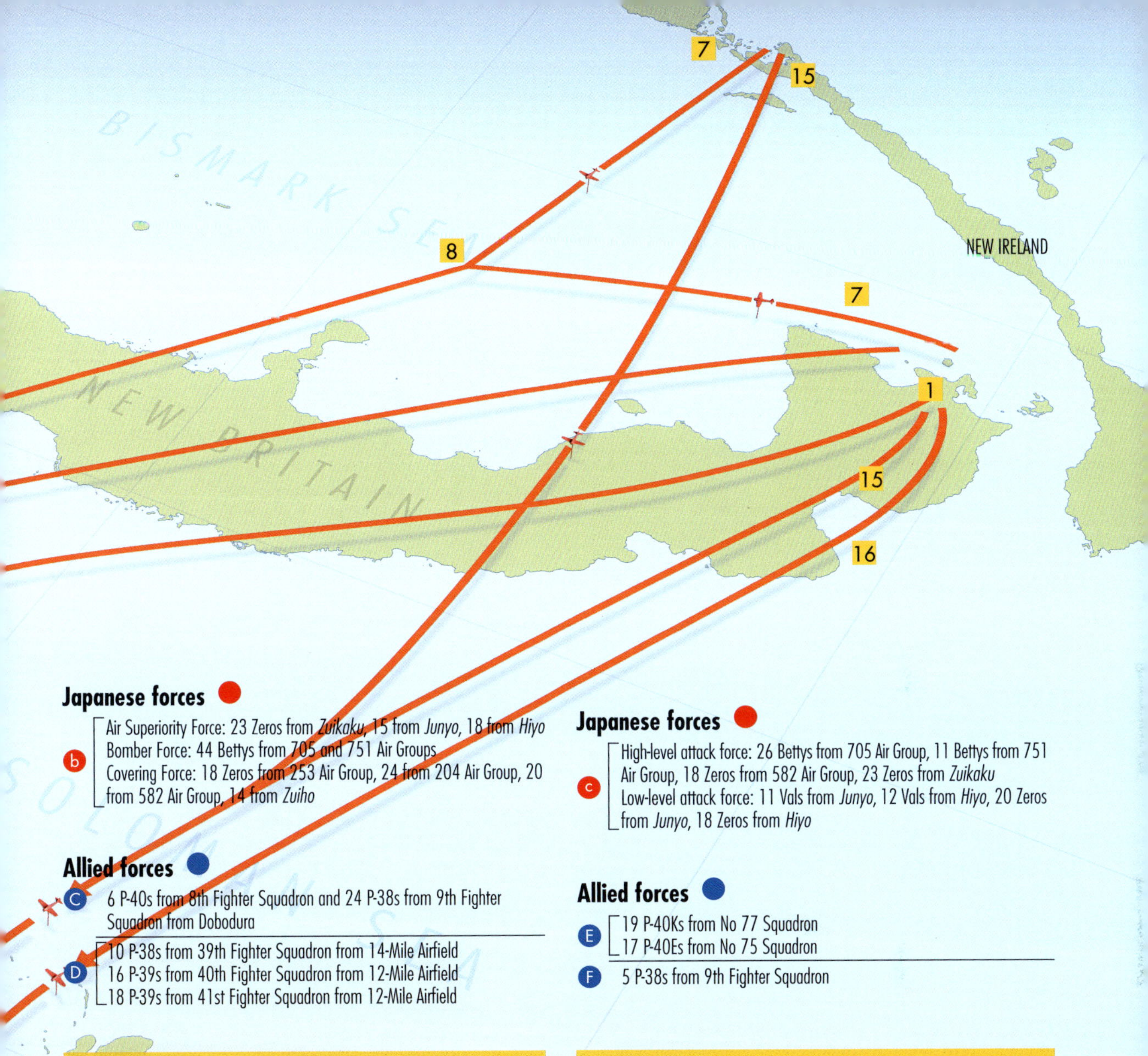

Japanese forces 🔴

B — Air Superiority Force: 23 Zeros from *Zuikaku*, 15 from *Junyo*, 18 from *Hiyo*
Bomber Force: 44 Bettys from 705 and 751 Air Groups
Covering Force: 18 Zeros from 253 Air Group, 24 from 204 Air Group, 20 from 582 Air Group, 14 from *Zuiho*

Japanese forces 🔴

C — High-level attack force: 26 Bettys from 705 Air Group, 11 Bettys from 751 Air Group, 18 Zeros from 582 Air Group, 23 Zeros from *Zuikaku*
Low-level attack force: 11 Vals from *Junyo*, 12 Vals from *Hiyo*, 20 Zeros from *Junyo*, 18 Zeros from *Hiyo*

Allied forces 🔵

C — 6 P-40s from 8th Fighter Squadron and 24 P-38s from 9th Fighter Squadron from Dobodura

D —
10 P-38s from 39th Fighter Squadron from 14-Mile Airfield
16 P-39s from 40th Fighter Squadron from 12-Mile Airfield
18 P-39s from 41st Fighter Squadron from 12-Mile Airfield

Allied forces 🔵

E —
19 P-40Ks from No 77 Squadron
17 P-40Es from No 75 Squadron

F — 5 P-38s from 9th Fighter Squadron

EVENTS (2)

April 12 – Attack on Port Moresby

7. 0610hrs. Japanese strike begins to launch.
8. 0745hrs. Japanese formation assembles and moves south at 22,000ft.
9. 0930hrs. First American fighters scramble.
10. 1000hrs. Japanese assume attack formation and head toward Port Moresby.
11. 1015hrs. P-38s from 39th Fighter Squadron begin to engage.
12. 1023–1026hrs. Bettys begin bomb runs at Port Moresby.
13. 1030hrs. Betty formation fragmented by fighter attack; six are shot down and another forced to crash-land.
14. After 1030hrs. Inconclusive fighter combat continues until Japanese reach the north coast of New Guinea.

EVENTS (3)

April 14 – Attack on Milne Bay

15. 0845–0900hrs. High-level attack force departs Kavieng and Rabaul.
16. 1000hrs. Low-level attack force departs.
17. 1107–1137hrs. Nos 77 and 75 Squadrons scramble.
18. 1230hrs. RAAF P-40s conduct frontal attack on Betty formation.
19. About 1230hrs. Bettys and Vals conduct bombing attack, inflicting some losses on Allied shipping.
20. 1230–1250hrs. Air combat results in three Allied fighters and three Zeros being lost.

I-Go called for attacks on Port Moresby airfields on April 12, 1943. Here, a fuel dump burns at Three Mile 'Drome after the attack. The Japanese also hit Five, 12, and 14 Mile 'Dromes, attempting to disrupt Allied airpower threatening Lae and Salamaua, losing seven Bettys that day. (NARA)

By 1030hrs, the tight Betty formation was fragmented and losses began to mount. Six bombers were sent spiraling down into the New Guinea jungle and a seventh was forced to crash-land at Lae. Opposing fighters continued a high-altitude duel from Port Moresby to the north coast of New Guinea. Even with the huge numbers of fighters in the fray, only two P-39Ds from the 41st Fighter Squadron and an 80th Fighter Squadron P-38F failed to return. No Zeros were lost.

After a day's rest, Yamamoto mounted *I-Go*'s final raid against shipping and Gurney strip at Milne Bay. It was planned as a joint strike from land-based 11th Air Fleet elements and carrier air units, but neither knew of the other's participation because of security concerns. As usual, the first aircraft to take off were two Dinahs for pre-strike reconnaissance and weather reports. The high-level strike included 37 Bettys from the 705 and 751 Air Groups. Six more bombers from 751 Air Group from Kavieng failed to make the trip after two collided and four aborted. The Bettys were covered by 18 Zeros from the 582 Air Group (two more aborted) and 23 from the *Zuikaku*. Vals from the *Hiyo* and *Junyo* formed the low-level attack force; these were covered by 18 Zeros from *Hiyo* and 20 from *Junyo*.

Based at Milne Bay were two RAAF fighter squadrons. With advance warning provided by radar, 18 Kittyhawks from No 77 Squadron scrambled first (another fighter was forced to abort), followed by another 17 Kittyhawks from No 75 Squadron. Just after noon on April 14, the combined Australian force spotted the approaching Japanese and began a frontal attack on the Betty formation. Two bombers were forced down on the first pass. Minutes after this opening attack, a single P-38, flown by rising star First Lieutenant Richard Bong – destined to become the top American ace of the entire war – made contact with the bombers. The 9th Fighter Squadron had launched eight P-38s, but three aborted and only Bong was able to make an intercept. He damaged two Bettys on his first pass, one of which later crash-landed at Gasmata. In his next pass, he shot down a Betty.

The Betty attack caused no damage to the airfield. They hit two ships in the bay, with a small Dutch merchantman being sunk and a small British merchant vessel suffering severe damage. All but three of the Vals survived fighter attacks, but with their 132lb bombs they lightly damaged only two Australian corvettes and a small Dutch cargo ship, partly due to strafing from Vals and Zeros.

In the concurrent dogfight, the Zeros claimed 44 kills – in fact they shot down only a single No 77 Squadron Kittyhawk, and a No 75 Kittyhawk was forced to crash-land and was subsequently written off. One P-38F was shot down by the Zeros covering the dive-bombers and its pilot killed. In return, the Japanese lost three Bettys, three Vals, and three Zeros (one from the *Zuikaku*, and two more from *Junyo* after they were forced to crash-land at Rabaul).

After only four attacks (one against Guadalcanal and three against targets on New Guinea), Yamamoto called off *I-Go*. Misled by the extravagant claims of his aviators against Allied aircraft in the air and on the ground, and against shipping, the Japanese had some optimism that the Allies' capability to begin offensive operations had been curtailed. In fact, the operation was a spectacular failure. Yamamoto's staff understood this when they tallied their losses, which came to 45 aircraft – 17 Zeros, 18 Vals, and ten Bettys over the course of only four raids. Had the Japanese been aware of the true scale of Allied losses – 30 aircraft and five ships, most insignificant – they would have been even more pessimistic. *I-Go* marked the high-water mark of Japanese airpower over New Guinea.

ANALYSIS AND CONCLUSION
An evaluation of Japanese airpower

The Japanese offensive air campaign in New Guinea was a profound disaster for the IGHQ's strategy, and for the IJNAF's combat capability. Japan's defeat in its goal of expanding and strengthening the southern portion of its defensive boundary grew out of mistaken strategic and operational decisions, reinforcing failure, and misallocation of already inadequate resources.

At the strategic level, the Japanese took too long to implement their plans in the South Pacific. The IGHQ and Combined Fleet tried to expand the defensive perimeter in too many places with inadequate resources. The Japanese simply misjudged the speed of the Allied defensive buildup, limited though it was. In May, Operation *MO* was mounted with only a fraction of the Combined Fleet's carrier force, and this commitment proved insufficient. Japan's defeat at Midway in June ended any hope that the Combined Fleet could use massed carrier airpower to achieve local air superiority long enough to seize and develop adequate airfields deeper in the South Pacific. While possession of Gasmata and the early March seizure of Lae and Salamaua provided IJNAF airfields closer to the target of Port Moresby, the Japanese failed to fully exploit this advantage. These airfields were never fully developed from the habitability, maintenance, or air defense standpoints to effectively support large numbers of aircraft. The failure to establish an effective early warning system for Lae was disastrous. Allied attacks on Lae effectively limited the IJNAF's capability by not only destroying and damaging aircraft, but by tying up fighters in continuous daylight defensive patrols. This diluted the 24th and 25th Flotillas' ability to concentrate forces against Allied airpower when it was at its weakest. Gaining Buna airfield completely failed to enhance the IJNAF's capabilities. It took several weeks after the July 21 invasion to bring it into use, only to have it available for about a month before it was abandoned in early September due to persistent Allied attacks.

Early in the campaign, Allied aircraft production and aircrew training lagged behind the Japanese. Despite the priority of the war in Europe, the Allies managed to ramp up the output of men and machines to match the Japanese, beginning about six months after Pearl Harbor. Though basically even numerically in aircraft with the Allies well into 1943, the Japanese

The Papua Hotel in Port Moresby was Brigadier General Whitehead's ADVON headquarters, from which he directed Allied air operations as Kenney's deputy from August 1942. The ADVON layer of operational command was one of several innovations by Kenney that allowed the most effective employment of limited Allied airpower. (NARA)

ANALYSIS AND CONCLUSION

The Allies salvage the Zero knocked out on August 26 at Buna (see p. 55) for technical exploitation after capturing the airfield in December. The IJNAF's efforts utterly failed to support effectively Japan's New Guinea campaign. During the campaign the IJNAF suffered debilitating losses and never effectively exploited the advantages it possessed in numbers, experience, and operational initiative. (NARA)

acceptance of an attritional air war was a losing strategy. This resulting decline of Japanese airpower was manifested not just in numbers but in the inexperience of the replacement IJNAF aircrews and ground personnel as 1942 progressed. Even when Japanese air units were at top proficiency at the start of the campaign, they lacked the power to suppress key Allied air facilities or exact heavy attrition during air battles. This inability to deliver a knockout blow was attributable to the low numbers of aircraft available and the characteristics of those aircraft. In particular, the Betty lacked the payload to suppress or destroy large facilities. Forced to fly at higher altitude to reduce losses, the accuracy of the Bettys was greatly reduced, further reducing their lethality. All of the shortcomings of Japanese airpower were intensified by a dispersion of effort. The Japanese sacrificed their efforts in New Guinea to deal with Guadalcanal, which spread available air assets too thinly and virtually ensured that neither campaign received adequate attention. It is worth noting that even when the IJNAF focused its main effort against American airpower operating from a single facility on Guadalcanal, it was similarly unable to gain any measure of air superiority. Against a larger Allied air force flying from a much larger number of facilities on New Guinea, it was very unlikely that the Japanese would enjoy any larger degree of success.

Operationally, the Japanese use of airpower in their New Guinea campaign reflected, and suffered from, both unrealistic expectations and irresolute pursuit of them. The 11th Air Fleet was defeated, having neither shaped the conditions for Japanese ground forces to capture Port Moresby and Milne Bay nor checked the growth of Allied airpower on New Guinea as the campaign wore on. Despite multiple waves of bomber and fighter reinforcements that the IJNAF moved into the theater – especially in April, August, and November – it never mounted sustained, effective bombing attacks against even the two Allied airfields at Port Moresby operational early in the campaign, Three Mile and Seven Mile 'Dromes, let alone the airfield and infrastructure buildup the Allies conducted over the second half of 1942.

The IJNAF also did not employ its long-range bombing capability to hold key Allied air bases in Australia – such as Horn Island, Cairns, and Garbutt – at sufficient risk to deny the Allies the operational benefits of building up American air units in these areas as the campaign wore on. Nor did the IJNAF ever seriously undertake to choke off Port Moresby from receiving supplies from Australia by sea, instead contenting themselves with high-altitude bombing attacks on Port Moresby town and its airfields that, except in a few instances, amounted to little more than nuisance raids. *I-Go*, the last operational-level Japanese offensive action, clearly exemplifies all these failings. It had no chance of success since it was poorly planned, being marked by poor target selection, dispersal of effort, and lack of follow-up. After 14 months of the grueling campaign the Japanese had still not digested the lesson that to be successful, airpower must be applied in a concerted manner over time, not in just a few decisive attacks.

The IJNAF also did not cooperate well with the IJA. Its conduct of reconnaissance, ground support, and supply operations for the Buna operation were far too sporadic and small-scale to affect the outcome of the ground campaign. Nor did the IJNAF coordinate operations particularly well with Japanese maritime transport operations generally. At Buna, the invasion force had to disembark during the first full day while dodging Allied attacks due to the IJNAF's inability or unwillingness to attempt operations in poor weather. The RAAF's destruction of Japanese transports at Milne Bay occurred without any interference from the IJNAF for similar reasons and was key to the Australian victory. At the battle of the Bismarck Sea, the covering fighters were poorly deployed. Flying at medium altitude, they were concerned with the heavy bombers – the Allied aircraft most able to defend themselves against fighter attack and those escorted by the P-38s. The real threat was the low-level attackers, which were ignored by the Japanese fighters until it was too late to save the convoy.

An evaluation of Allied airpower

The Allied strategy of holding on in New Guinea despite the lack of resources proved a successful gamble. They benefited greatly from the lackadaisical manner in which the IJNAF conducted the campaign early on and its virtual abandonment of New Guinea operations in September and October. The Allies also understood that since Rabaul was the Japanese center of gravity, it had to be struck consistently, regardless of their limited capability to do so. Allied bombing against both airfields and shipping at Rabaul rarely bore significant results owing to the small numbers of attacking aircraft, bad weather, and misapplied doctrine, and was ultimately limited primarily to nighttime missions. However, it did have the effect of inflicting costs on the Japanese in terms of destroyed or damaged equipment and supplies, frequent runway repair, and allocation of already limited aircraft and antiaircraft artillery to its defense. The Japanese were thus denied Rabaul as a fully secure area from which to launch offensive action. The Allied strategy of waging a counter-air campaign, fighting the IJNAF at every opportunity despite unfavorable odds, kept them in the fight until more units, with better aircraft, began reaching the theater.

Early in the campaign, Allied bombing doctrine for medium and dive-bombers was virtually lacking, and commanders and crews had to learn while doing, accounting for some of the negative results during this period. Heavy bombers were likewise misemployed against maritime targets, especially those underway, by conducting level bombing from high altitudes. Though truly strategic targets except for Rabaul were lacking in this campaign, the Allies could have better used their limited number of Catalinas, B-17s, and B-24s to bomb land targets rather than Japanese combat and transport shipping. The arrival of Allied medium bombers – first B-26s and later Beaufighters, Bostons, Beauforts, B-25Cs, and A-20As – to support the limited RAAF Catalina and Hudson inventory allowed the Allies to implement more effective attacks against Japanese surface vessels.

Allied doctrinal and tactical flexibility also played a key role in turning the tide in the campaign in late 1942. The shift to medium- and low-altitude bombing, and the development of skip bombing, even by B-17s, as well as the modification of B-25s and A-20s/Bostons for both strafing and dropping of parafrag bomblets, combined with the close coordination of bombing and strafing attacks from different altitudes and times to confuse or overwhelm

No 30 Squadron Beaufighters began operations from Five Mile 'Drome on September 17, that day strafing barges and supply dumps at Buna–Sanananda, an attack MacArthur called "a honey." The unit racked up a sterling record during the Buna fighting and later played an exemplary role in the Bismarck Sea action. (Claringbould)

Japanese defenses. Several Allied attacks against Lae airfield and Buna resupply efforts in late 1942 displayed this sophisticated orchestration of airpower.

At the battle of the Bismarck Sea, these doctrinal and tactical evolutions were brought to a terrible perfection. During the battle, 253 1,000lb and 261 500lb bombs were dropped from bombers conducting horizontal attacks. Of these, 30 hits were claimed for an 8 percent success rate. The actual rate was much less than the 30 claimed hits. Skip-bombers dropped 137 bombs, with 48 claimed as hits. Though 48 hits was an exaggeration, what is undeniable was that 18 low-level B-25s and 12 A-20s hit three destroyers and seven transports in the span of 15 minutes on the morning of March 3. The 12 B-25s dedicated for mast-height attacks and 12 A-20s claimed a success rate of 46 percent; the six conventional B-25s attacking at low level achieved a 17 percent success rate. The Allies had turned from a nuisance in attacking surface ships to a lethal threat, even against the previously invulnerable destroyers.

During the land campaign, the adroit use of air transport to improve the mobility and supply of land forces was probably the single most effective aspect of the Allied air effort. Though the number of purpose-built military transport aircraft was never large during 1942, the Allies' dedication to use transports to get troops to the Kokoda, Buna, and Wau fronts quickly, and to supplement the limited number of US C-47s with US B-17s and LB-30s, and RAAF Hudsons and smaller transports – as well as with co-opted Australian civilian aircraft – was cited by Kenney's own deputy chief of staff as the most significant air forces contribution to the defeat of the Japanese in Papua.

Finally, despite the long distances and transportation problems both between the US and Australia and within Australia itself, the Allied ability to provide, assemble, repair, and modify aircraft from the relative safety of reasonably well-appointed Australian facilities was a huge advantage. The Japanese were also able to replace aircraft by flying and shipping them between Japan and Rabaul, but did not have the same level of repair and maintenance facilities as close to the front as the Allies. In this sense, the operational-level "interior lines" factor favored the Allies.

For the reasons cited above, Japan's New Guinea air campaign seemed almost inevitably doomed to failure. The Japanese could never decide exactly how they wanted to proceed in the South Pacific, and in any event mustered too few resources and applied them in too desultory a fashion to succeed. The Allies, laser focused on keeping the Japanese away from the Australian mainland, were thereby better able to direct their more limited forces to deny Japan yet another cheap victory. The stage was thus set for the Allies' own New Guinea air campaign.

BIBLIOGRAPHY

Air Command and Staff College, *Airpower Employment of the Fifth Air Force in the World War II Southwest Pacific Theater*, Creative Space Publishers Platform, Middletown, DE (2014)

Bergerud, Eric M., *Fire in the Sky*, Westview Press, Boulder, CO (2000)

Bullard, Steven (trans.), *Japanese Army Operations in the South Pacific Area*, Australian War Memorial, Canberra, Australia (2007)

Carter, Kit C. & Mueller, Robert, *The Army Air Forces in World War II: Combat Chronology 1941–1945*, Office of Air Force History, Washington, DC (1973)

Claringbould, Michael John, *A6M2/3 Zero-sen: New Guinea and the Solomons 1942*, Osprey Publishing, New York, NY (2023)

Claringbould, Michael John, *P-39/P-400 Airacobra vs A6M2/3 Zero-sen I New Guinea 1942*, Osprey Publishing, New York, NY (2018)

Claringbould, Michael John, *Operation I-GO*, Avonmore Books, Kent Town, Australia (2020)

Claringbould, Michael, *South Pacific Air War, Vol 1: The Fall of Rabaul December 1941–March 1942*, Avonmore Books, Kent Town, Australia (2017)

Claringbould, Michael, *South Pacific Air War, Vol 2: The Struggle for Moresby March–April 1942*, Avonmore Books, Kent Town, Australia (2018)

Claringbould, Michael, *South Pacific Air War, Vol 3: Coral Sea & Aftermath May–June 1942*, Avonmore Books, Kent Town, Australia (2019)

Claringbould, Michael, *South Pacific Air War, Vol 4: Buna and Milne Bay June–September 1942*, Avonmore Books, Kent Town, Australia (2020)

Claringbould, Michael, *South Pacific Air War, Vol 5: Crisis in Papua September–December 1942*, Avonmore Books, Kent Town, Australia (2022)

Cooper, Anthony, *Kokoda Air Strikes*, NewSouth Publishing, Sydney, Australia (2014)

Craven, W. F. & Cate, J. L. (eds), *The Army Air Forces in World War II, Vol. I: Plans and Early Operations January 1939 to August 1942*, Office of Air Force History, Washington, DC (1983)

Craven, W. F. & Cate, J. L. (eds), *The Army Air Forces in World War II, Vol. IV: The Pacific – Guadalcanal to Saipan*, University of Chicago Press, Chicago, IL (1950)

Drea, Edward J., *MacArthur's ULTRA*, University Press of Kansas, Lawrence, KS (1992)

Gamble, Bruce, *Fortress Rabaul*, Zenith Press, Minneapolis, MN (2010)

General Headquarters, Far East Command, Military Intelligence Section, *Japanese Monograph No. 122 (Navy): Outline of Southeast Area Air Operations Part III Nov 42 – Jun 43*, Washington, DC (1950)

Gillison, Douglas, *Royal Australian Air Force 1939–1942*, Australian War Memorial, Canberra, Australia (1962)

Griffith, Thomas E. Jr, *MacArthur's Airman*, University Press of Kansas, Lawrence, KS (1998)

Hata, Ikuhiko & Izawa, Yasuho, *Japanese Naval Aces and Fighter Units in World War II*, Naval Institute Press, Annapolis, MD (1989)

Hata, Ikuhiko, Izawa, Yasuho & Shores, Christopher, *Japanese Army Air Force Fighter Units and Their Aces 1931–1945*, Grub Street, London, UK (2002)

Headquarters, US Far East Command, Military History Section, *Japanese Monograph No. 96: Eastern New Guinea Invasion Operations*, Department of the Army, Washington, DC (1953)

Kenney, George C., *General Kenney Reports*, Office of Air Force History, Washington, DC (1987)

BIBLIOGRAPHY

Maloney, Edward T. (ed), *Fighter Tactics of the Ace's S.W.P.A.*, World War II Publications, Corona Del Mar, CA (1978)

Maurer, Maurer (ed), *Combat Squadrons of the Air Force, World War II*, Office of Air Force History, Washington, DC (1982)

Milner, Samuel, *Victory in Papua*, Center of Military History, Washington, DC (1989)

Odgers, George, *Air War against Japan 1943–1945*, Australian War Memorial, Canberra, Australia (1968)

Richard L. Watson Papers, Rubenstein Library, Duke University, Durham, NC

Rust, Kenn C., *Fifth Air Force Story*, Historical Aviation Album, Temple City, CA (1973)

United States Air Force Historical Studies: No 86, *Close Air Support in the War against Japan*, Air University, Maxwell AFB, AL (1955)

United States Strategic Bombing Survey, *The Fifth Air Force in the War against Japan*, Alpha Editions, n. p. (2020)

Veitch, Michael, *44 Days*, Hachette, Sydney, Australia (2017)

Veitch, Michael, *Turning Point*, Hachette, Sydney, Australia (2022)

INDEX

Note: page numbers in bold refer to photographs, illustrations and captions.

accidents and mechanical problems 19, **22,** 30, 41, 42, 44, 52, 53, 63, **70**
Adachi, Gen Hatazo 83
air group numbering nomenclature 11, **11**
air superiority 47, 89, 90
air transport 23, **30,** 64–66, **65, 76,** 92
aircraft 32, 44, 46, 48
  Aichi D3A1 "Val" (Japan) 13, **28,** 49, 53, 54, **(55)56–57, 58, 58, 59,** 64, **(67)68–69,** 71, 72, 73, 85, **86, 87,** 88
  Bell P-39 (US) 22, **22, 23,** 36, 37, 38, 41, 42, 43, **44,** 45, 46, 47, 58, 70, 76, **76,** 88
  Bell P-400 (US) 22, 44, 45, 46, **46,** 47, 48, 49, **49,** 54, 55, 58, 59, 62, 70, 76
  Boeing B-17 (US) 21, 23, 43, **55,** 77, **79,** 80, 81, 82, 83–84, 91, 92
    B-17D 51
    B-17E 30, 31, **31,** 32, 33, 35, 37, 38, 39–40, 41–42, 44, 45, 46, 47, 48, 49, 51, **51,** 52–53, 55, 63, 64, 70, 72
    B-17F 51, **51,** 52–53, 55, 61, 63, 64, 70, 71, 72, **(73)74–75**
  Bristol Beaufighter (RAAF) 19, 21, 61, 64, 70, 77, **79,** 81, **81,** 82, 83, **83,** 85, 91, **92**
  Bristol Beaufort (RAAF) 19, **45,** 45–46, 61, 77, 81, 82, 91
  CAC Wirraway (RAAF) 19, 41, 42, 70, **71,** 76
  Consolidated B-24D (US) 9, 21, 63, **64,** 77, **79,** 80, 81, 91
    LB-30 (export) 21, 23, 47, 58, 92
  Consolidated PBY Catalina (US) 19, 28–30, 31, **32,** 33, 40, 45, 46, 47, 49, 63, **79,** 81, 91
  Curtiss P-40 Kittyhawk (RAAF) 8, **9,** 17, 19, 22, **22,** 34, 35, 36, 37, 38, 39, 40, 41, 42, 43, 48, **49,** 54, **(55)56–57,** 57–58, **58,** 59, **61,** 70, 72, **72,** 73, 85, **86, 87,** 88
  Douglas A-20 Boston (US) 19, 19–21, **22,** 51, **52,** 60–61, 64, 70, **70, 79,** 81, 82, 83, 91, 92
  Douglas A-24 (US) 21, 36, 37, 38, **39,** 40, 41, 43, 47, 51
  Kawanishi H6K "Mavis" (Japan) **24,** 28, 33, 39, 42, 43, 45
  Kawasaki Ki-48 "Lily" (Japan) 16, 76
  Lockheed A-29 Hudson (RAAF) 19, 28, **30,** 31, 32–33, 34–35, 41, 46, 47, 51, 52, 54, 58, 59, 64, 91, 92
  Lockheed C-47 (US) 23, 64, 65, **65,** 72, 76, **76,** 92
  Lockheed P-38F (US) 9, 22, **22,** 72–73, **73,** 77, 80, 81, 82, 83, 85, **86, 87,** 88, 91
    F-4A variant 22, 42, 61
  Martin B-26 (US) 21–22, 36, 37, **37,** 38, 39–40, **40,** 41, 42, 43, **44,** 45, 46, 47, 48, **48,** 49, **50,** 51, 55, 58, 59, 70, 91
  Mitsubishi A5M "Claude" (Japan) 28, 30–31, 37, 39, 42
  Mitsubishi A6M Zero "Zeke" (Japan) 11, 12–13, **13,** 15, **15,** 16, 19, 22, **25,** 28, 30–31, 32–33, 34, 35, 36, **36,** 37, 38, 39, 40, 41, 42, 43, 44, 45, 46, 47, 48, 49, 51, 52, 53, 54, 55, **(55)56–57, 58,** 58–59, 61, **61,** 62, 64, 71, 72, **(73)74–75,** 76, **79,** 80, 81, 82, 85, **86,** 88, **90**
    A6M3 "Hamp" 13, 49, 53, **55**
  Mitsubishi C5M2 "Babs" (Japan) 35, 44, 46, 52
  Mitsubishi G3M "Nell" (Japan) 13, 28, 31, 35, 39, 42, 43, **43,** 44, 45
  Mitsubishi G4M1 "Betty" (Japan) **10,** 12, 28, 31, 33–34, **34,** 35, **35,** 36, 37, 38, 39, 40, 41, 42–43, **43,** 46, 47, 48, 49, 51, 52, 53, 61, 62, 63–64, 72, 77, 84–85, **87,** 88, **88,** 90
  Mitsubishi Ki-46 "Dinah" (Japan) 16, 85, 88
  Nakajima Ki-27 (Japan) 15, 16
  Nakajima Ki-43 "Oscar" (Japan) 15, **15,** 16, 22, 64, 72, 73, 76, 81, 83
  North American B-25C (US) 21–22, 36, 37, **37,** 38, 40, 42, 43, 44, 45, 46, 47, 49, 55, 61, 70, **79, 80,** 81, **81,** 82, 83, 84, 85, 91, 92
airfields and bases 5, 7, 8, **13, 14,** 16, 23, 25, 27, **29,** 51–52, 85, **88,** 89, **90**
  14 Mile 'Drome 39, 42, **42,** 44, 61, **62,** 67, 70, 72, **72, 73,** 88
  Lae **25,** 31–32, 34–35, 38, 44, 49, **50,** 51, 64, 89
  Rabaul, New Britain 4, 8, 11, 12, **14,** 16, 30, 63, 91
  Salamaua 46, 49
  Seven Mile 'Drome 37, **37,** 38, 39, 40, **40,** 41, **41,** 42, 43, **44,** 45, 46, **46,** 47, 48, **49,** 51, 65
  Vunakanau 16, 31, 33, **34,** 35, **35,** 37, 38, 40, 41, 51, 52, 53, 63
  Wau 76
Allied Air Forces Headquarters, the 8, 18
Allied strategy and actions 4, 5, 18, 25, 26, 27, 30–31, 32, 33, 34, 36, 37–38, **39, 40,** 41, 42, 43–44, 45–46, 47, 49, **50,** 51, **51,** 52, **54, 55,** 55–58, 59, **60,** 60–61, **62,** 63–73, **71, 72,** 77–80, **78–79, 81,** 81–83, **82,** 89, **92**
  and bombing doctrine 91–92
antiaircraft fire 19, 23, 30, 33, 34, 35, 37, 40, 46, **48,** 51, 55, 58, 59, 62, **62,** 76, 82, 83
armor protection **10,** 12, 13, 15
Australian Army, the 25, 43–44, 46, 51, 52, 58, 59, 65, 66, 67, 76
  Kanga Force 26, 44, 76

Battle of Midway (June 1942), the 8, 24, 89
Battle of Milne Bay (August 1942), the 9, 25, **26,** 27, 53–60, **54, (55)56–57, 58**
Battle of the Bismarck Sea (March 1943), the 9, 77–84, **78–79, 80, 81, 82, 83, 84,** 91, 92, **92**
Battle of the Coral Sea (May 1942) 8, 27, 42
bomb payloads **10,** 12, 13, 16, 19, 21, 22, **24, 31, 37, 43,** 72, 90
bombing accuracy 30, 38, 41, 42, 43, 51, 90
Bong, First Lt Richard 88
Bostock, Air Vice-Marshal William **(16)17,** 18, 60
Brett, Lt Gen George **(16)17,** 18, 60
Buna invasion, the 47–49, **49,** 51
Buna-Sanananda-Gona defense complex, the 27, **63,** 67, 70, **71,** 72

camouflage 54, 70
CAPs (combat air patrols) 77, **79,** 80, 81, 82
close air support 58, 67–70
crash-landings 31, 39, 40, 41, 42, 43, 44, 45, **48,** 55, 62, 73, 83, 88

deaths 16, 30, 34, 35, **35,** 37, 38, 39, 40, 41, 42, 43, 44, 45, 46, 47, 48, 49, 53, 54, 55, **58,** 59, **67, 79,** 80, 83, 84, **84**
  and international law 84

DEI campaign, the 4, 5, 16
destroyer escorts 71–72, 73, **73,** 77
dogfights **17,** 19, 34, 35, 40, 42, 46, **46,** 53, **(55)56–57,** 76, 88

fighter aces 11, **36,** 88
fighter escorts 37, 38, 39, 41, 42–43, 44, 45, 49, **49,** 51, 52, **(55)56–57,** 58, 61, 62, 70, **72,** 76, **76,** 91
fighter sweeps 35, 39, 40, 41, 42, 43, 45, 46
fuel dumps 34, 38, 40, **40,** 47, **88**

Garing, Capt William "Bull" 18, 60, **60**
Gasmata bombing raid 30–31
Guadalcanal campaign, the 9, 10, 11, 12, 16, 24, 25, 49, 52, 53, 90

Harding, Maj Gen Edwin **67**
Hewitt, Air Commodore J. E. 18

IGHQ (Imperial General Headquarters), the 24, 26, 47, 89
IJA (Imperial Japanese Army), the 8, 13, 15, 24, 31, 73, 77, 84, 91
  6th Air Division 15
  17th Army 9, 10, 47, 51
  18th Army 11, 26, 83
  21st Mixed Independent Brigade 72
  51st Division 73, 77
  Eighth Area Army 10
  South Seas Force 8, 24, 25, 62, 65, 66, 67, 70, 71
  Yokoyama Advance Force 24–25, 47, 49
IJAAF (Imperial Japanese Army Air Force), the 4, 9, 13–16, **25,** 76
  12th Air Brigade 16
  76th Independent Reconnaissance Squadron 16
  regiments
    1st **15,** 16
    11th **15,** 16, 72, 76, 81, 83
    45th 16, 76
IJN (Imperial Japanese Navy), the 13, 15, 24, 31, 47, 53, 77
  4th Fleet 24
  8th Fleet 47
  Combined Fleet 10, 89
  Destroyer Squadron 3 10, 77, **79,** 83
  ships 12, **48,** 71–72, **79,** 83, 88
    Arashio (destroyer) **79,** 83, 84, **84**
    Asagumo (destroyer) 80
    Asanagi (destroyer) 47
    Asashio (destroyer) **79,** 83
    Ayotosan Maru (transport) 47
    Kembu Maru (transport) **79,** 80, 83, **83**
    Kiyokawa Maru (seaplane tender) 32
    Komaki Maru (transport) 38
    Kotoku Maru (carrier) 47
    Kyokusei Maru (transport) 80
    Nojima (transport) 81, 83, 84
    Tokitsukaze (destroyer) **79,** 83, 84, **84**
    Yokohama Maru (transport) 32
    Yukikaze (destroyer) 80, 83
    Zuiho (carrier) 12, 77, 82
SNLF (Special Naval Landing Forces) 24, 31, 53, 58, **58,** 59, 60, 73, 77, 84
  Sasebo 5th 53, 54

INDEX

IJNAF (Imperial Japanese Navy Air Force), the 4, 5, 8, 9, 11, 15, 16, **25,** 47–48, **55,** 60, 61, **84,** 89, 90, **90,** 91
   11th Air Fleet 11, 12, **13, 28, 34,** 35, **35,** 39, **43, 50, 59,** 61, 62, **62,** 65, **(67)68–69,** 72, **85,** 88, 90
   Air Flotillas
      21st 11, 28
      24th 8, 11, 28, 31, 33, 35, 89
      25th 8, 11, 35, 36–37, 39, 41, 42, 43, 44, 45, 46, 47, 49, 51, 52, 53, 58, 59, 89
      26th 11, 49, 53
   Air Groups 11, 61, 62
      1st 28, 31, 35, 36
      2nd 11, 49, 51, 53, 54, 55, **55,** 59, **59,** 62
      3rd 61, 62
      4th **10,** 11, 16, 28, 30–31, 32, 33, 34, 35, 36, **36, 40, 46,** 47, 51, 52, 53, 61–62
      14th 11, 48
      204 (6th) 11, **11,** 12, 61, 62, **79**
      251 (Tainan) 11, **11,** 12, **25,** 35–36, **36,** 37, 38, 39–40, 43, 44, 46, 47, 48, 49, 51, 52, 53, **55,** 58
      252 (Genzan) **11,** 12, 42, **43,** 64, 72, **79**
      253 (Kanoya fighters) 11, **11,** 12, 61, 62, 77, **79,** 80
      582 **11,** 12, 64, **(67)68–69,** 71, 72, **73,** 88
      705 (Misawa) 11, **11,** 51, 61, 62, 72
      751 (Kanoya Bombers) **11,** 62, 63–64, 77, 88
      Kisarazu 36, 53, 62
      Yokohama 28, 36, 42, 43, 44
   Attack Air Forces 39, 42, 62
Imamura, Lt Gen Hitoshi 10–11, 73
intelligence 41, **42,** 47, 52, 53, **59,** 71, 77
intercepts 12, 13, 16, 22, 30, 31, 34, 35, 38, 39, 40, **44,** 48, 49, 51, 52, **62, 79,** 81, 88
Itahana, Lt Gen Güchi 15

Jackson, Squadron Ldr John 38, 40
Japanese strategy and actions 4–5, 8, 11–12, 15, 24–26, 28, 31–34, **34,** 35, 37, 38–40, 41, 42, 44–45, 46, 47–48, 49, **50,** 51, 52, 53–55, 58, 59–60, 61–62, 64, 65, **(67)68–69,** 70, 71, 72–77, 81, 82, 84–91, **85, 86–87, 88,** 92
Johnson, Lyndon 44
Jones, Air Vice-Marshal George 18

Kenney, Maj Gen George 8, 9, 18, 49, 52, 60, **60,** 63, 67, 70, 71, 77, **80,** 81, 85, **89**
kill claims 16, 33, 40, 58, 76, 80, 82, 83–84, 88, 92
Kimura, Rear Adm Masatomi 10, **12,** 77, 81, 83
Kokoda Trail, the 8, 9, 25, 27, 62
Kusaka, Vice-Adm Jinichi 10

logistics and supply 5, 25, 60, 62, 64, **65,** 65–66, **67,** 70, 71
   supply convoys 12, **12,** 16, 49, **52,** 71–72, **(73)74–75,** 73–76
      Lae resupply convoy (March 1943) 77–84, **78–79, 80, 81, 82, 83, 84**

MacArthur, Gen Douglas 5, 17, 18, 27, 47, 51, 66, 67, **92**
maintenance **23,** 32, 34, 39, 59, 92
Marston mats (PSP) 23, **54**
matèriel losses **10,** 11, 12, 16, 24, 28–30, 32, 33, 34, 35, 36, 37, 38, 39, **39,** 40, 41, 42, 43, **43,** 44, 45, 46, 47, 49, 52, 54, **55, 58, 59,** 60, 61, 65, 73, 76, **79,** 80, 82–83, **83,** 84, **84,** 85, 88, **88**
military strength and complements 12, 19, **20,** 28, 35, 39, 42, 43, 90

New Guinea theater (map) **6, 14**
New Guinea Volunteer Rifles militia 32

night operations 30, 31, 43, 45–46, 47, 48, 51, 63, **64,** 91

operational readiness 12, 21, **23, 35,** 59
Operations
   I-Go (April 1943) 9, **9,** 85–88, **86–87, 88,** 91
   MO (May 1942) 24, 39, 41, 42, 89
   RE (July 1942) 24–25, **26(27),** 62
   SR (March 1942) 24, 28, 31
orders of battle **36, 66, 78**
organizational and command structures 10–11, 13–15, **16,** 17–18, 60, 62, **89**
Oro Bay air raid, the **(67)68–69,** 71

Papua Hotel, Port Moresby **89**
pilot experience 11, 16, 17, 37, **42,** 43, 53, 61, 84, 90, **90**
Port Moresby 4, **5,** 8, **24,** 24–25, 34, 39, 42–43, **43,** 44, 45, **46,** 47, 48, 58, 62, 85, **88,** 89, 90

RAAF (Royal Australian Air Force), the 8, **16,** 17–18, 23, 30, 32, 34, 59, 60, 70, 71, 77, 91
   14th Reconnaissance Squadron 32
   No 1 Rescue and Communications Flight 58, 64–65
   No 9 Operational Group 18, 60, **60,** 61
   No 37 Radar Station 52, 53
   squadrons
      No 4 19, **71,** 76
      No 6 **30,** 52, 54, 58, 59, 64
      No 11 19, **32,** 45, 64, 81
      No 20 19, **32,** 64
      No 22 19, **19,** 70, **70,** 76, 83
      No 24 19, 41, 42
      No 30 19, 61, 76, 81, **81,** 82, 92
      No 32 19, 30, **30,** 31, 32, 48, 51, 52, 64
      No 75 8, **17,** 19, 34, 35, 36, 37, 38, 39, 41, 42, 44, 48, 52, 53, 54, **54, 55,** 55–58, **58,** 59, 61, **87, 88**
      No 76 8, 19, 48, **49,** 52, 53, 54, **54,** 58, **58,** 59, 61
      No 77 19, **86, 87,** 88
      No 100 19, 45, **45,** 61, 81
radar systems 52, 85, 88
radio communications 13, 54
Ramey, Brig Gen Howard K. 18
Ramey, Col Roger 18
ranges 5, **10,** 12, 13, 19, 21–22, 23, **24, 31,** 90
reconnaissance 8, 16, 21, 30, **30,** 32, **32,** 33, 34, 36, 38, 39, 40, 41, 42, 44, 46, 47, 48, 49, 52, 53, 59, 63, 64, 77
revetments 16, 23
Royal Australian Navy, the 49
runway maintenance 23

Sakai, Lt Saburo 36
Salamaua and Lae landings 31–33
sea rescues 30, **32,** 37, 40, 41, 49, 53, 54, 83, 84
self-sealing fuel tanks 12, 13
Simpson Harbor, Rabaul **51,** 63
"skip" bombing 61, 63, 82, 83, 91, 92
Solomons campaign, the 63
sorties 33, 58, 63, 67, 70, 76
spare parts **35,** 38
speed and performance 12–13, 15, 19, 21, 22, 38, **61**

Taijun Maru (merchant ship) 38
target identification 70
terrain 5, 7, 22, 27, **37,** 65, 70
training 18, 33, **45, 64,** 89
Tsukahara, Vice-Adm Nishizo 10, 62

US Army, the 51, 52, 62, 66
   32nd Infantry Division 25, 66, 67, **(67)68–69,** 71, **71**

US Marines, the 8
US Navy, the 30, 32, **45,** 47
   carriers 8, 30, 31, 32, 33
USAAF, the 4, 8, 18, 51, 59, 60, 77
   5th Air Force 9, 18, **52,** 60, 76
   8th Fighter Control Squadron 52
   8th Photo Reconnaissance Squadron 22, 42, **42,** 61
   104th Antiaircraft Battalion 23
   374th Troop Carrier Group 23, 65, 76
   709th Antiaircraft Machine Gun Battery 23
   745th Antiaircraft Battalion 23
   ADVON (Advanced Echelon) 18, 60, **89**
      5th 67
   Bomb Groups
      3rd 21, 22, **22,** 36, **37,** 38, **39,** 40, 42, 46, 51, **55,** 60–61, 81, 83
      19th 21, **31,** 33, 35, 36, 39, 40, 45, 47, 49, **51,** 52, 58, 63
      22nd 21, 36, **41,** 46, **48, 50,** 55, 58, 59, 70
      38th 61, 81
      43rd 18, **31,** 61, **64,** 72, **(73)74–75,** 83
      90th 21, 63, **64**
   Bomb Squadrons 36, 48, 70, 77, 81, 82
      8th 36, **39**
      13th **37,** 82
      14th 30, 33
      40th 33, 47
      63rd 61, 63, **79,** 80
      64th 63, 71, 81
      65th **79,** 80
      89th **22,** 51, **52,** 60–61, 82
      90th 22, **37, 80, 81,** 82, 83
      320th 63, **77,** 81
      321st 77, **79**
      435th 47, 54
   Fighter Groups
      8th 22, **23,** 36, 37–38, 41, 42, 43, 44, **44,** 48, 49, 52, 54, 61
      35th 22, **22,** 44, 48, 54, 76, **76**
      49th **9,** 22, 34, 61, **61,** 71, 72, **72,** 73, 76
   Fighter Squadrons **23,** 86
      7th 34, 61, **61,** 71, **86**
      8th 61, **86**
      9th **9,** 61, 77, 82, 88
      35th **23,** 41
      36th **23,** 41
      39th **22,** 44, 46, **46,** 48, 72–73, **73,** 82, **87**
      40th 44, 48
      41st 48, **49,** 58, 88
      80th 48, 54–55, 59, 88
   Troop Carrier Squadrons **23,** 64, 86
      6th 64, 76
      21st 43–44, 64, 67

Walker, Brig Gen Kenneth 18
weaponry 12, 13, 15, 16, 19–21, 22, 23, **41, 45,** 54, **70, 72,** 82
   23lb parafrag bomblet (US) **19,** 21, **22,** 51, 61, 70, 91
   100lb fragmentation bomb (US) 38
   132lb anti-personnel bomb (Japan) 39, 41, 58, 85, 88
   500lb bomb (US) 38, 42, **49,** 53, 64, 71, **73,** 82, 92
   551lb bomb (Japan) 85
   Bofors 40mm gun 23, 58, **62**
weather conditions 5–7, 22, 30, 32, 33, **37,** 42, 43, 46, 47, **48, 48,** 53, **55, 58, 59,** 60, 64, 65, 71, **73,** 76, 77, 81, 82, 83, 91
Whitehead, Brig Gen Ennis 18, 60, **60,** 67, 70, 71, 77, **89**
Wurtsmith, Brig Gen Paul 18

Yamamoto, Adm Isoroku 10, 11, 12, 84, 85, **85, 86,** 88